Banking Union as a Shock Absorber

Banking Union as a Shock Absorber

Lessons for the eurozone from the US

Daniel Gros and Ansgar Belke

Centre for European Policy Studies (CEPS), Brussels
Rowman & Littlefield International, London

Published by Rowman & Littlefield International, Ltd.
Unit A, Whitacre Mews, 26-34 Stannary Street, London SE11 4AB
www.rowmaninternational.com

Rowman & Littlefield International Ltd. is an affiliate of Rowman &
Littlefield
4501 Forbes Boulevard, Suite 200, Lanham, Maryland 20706, USA
With additional offices in Boulder, New York, Toronto (Canada), and
Plymouth (UK)
www.rowman.com

Centre for European Policy Studies
Place du Congrès 1, B-1000 Brussels
Tel: (32.2) 229.39.11 Fax: (32.2) 219.41.51
E-mail: info@ceps.eu
Website: http://www.ceps.eu

British Library Cataloguing in Publication Data
A catalogue record for this book is available from the British Library

ISBN: HB 978-1-78348-594-9
ISBN: PB 978-1-78348-595-6

⊖™ The paper used in this publication meets the minimum
requirements of American National Standard for Information
Sciences—Permanence of Paper for Printed Library Materials,
ANSI/NISO Z39.48-1992.

Printed in the United States of America

TABLE OF CONTENTS

Boxes, Figures and Tables

LIST OF ABBREVIATIONS

BRRD	bank resolution and recovery Directive
BU	banking union
CEBS	Committee of European Banking Supervisors
DGS	deposit guarantee scheme
EA	euro area
EBA	European Bank Authority
ECB	European Central Bank
EFSF	European Financial Stability Facility
EIP	excessive imbalances procedure
EMU	Economic and Monetary Union
EReIF	European Reinsurance Fund
ESM	European Stability Mechanism
ESRB	European Systemic Risk Board
FDIC	Federal Deposit Insurance Corporation
GDP	gross domestic product
GSEs	government-sponsored enterprises
GSP	gross state product
IGA	intergovernmental agreement
IMF	International Monetary Fund
LTV	loan-to-value (ratios)
MBS	mortgage-backed securities
RMBS	residential mortgage-backed securities
S&L	savings and loan
SIFIs	significantly important financial institutions
SRF	Single Resolution Fund
SRM	Single Resolution Mechanism
SSM	Single Supervisory Mechanism

PREFACE

The inspiration for this study came from the observation that the United States and Europe initially seemed to face a very similar financial crisis. Housing prices and credit had increased by a similar percentage on both sides of the Atlantic during the boom years which ended in 2007-08. The economic contraction and the tensions in financial markets also seemed very similar. However, after about 2009-10, the US started to recover, albeit slowly, with financial markets stabilising early on. In the euro area, by contrast, the crisis became a regional one, with pockets of concentrated tensions and large risk premia on government debt even in countries whose budgets had been in surplus before the crisis (Ireland and Spain).

This eruption of regional financial crisis seemed odd given that the preceding boom had also been regionally concentrated in the US. The extraordinary housing price booms in parts of the 'sun belt' of the US seemed to have been no different from what had happened in Ireland and Spain.

This difference suggested that it might be useful to study in detail how regional financial boom-bust cycles played out in the US. The results of this investigation proved to be both interesting and full of policy implications.

We gratefully acknowledge valuable comments received by participants at the "International Finance and Banking (FIBA) Conference, 26-27 March 2015 in Bucharest, where the background study to this book was presented as a keynote lecture.

Other useful comments were received at conferences in Tübingen, 7-8 May 2015 and Rethymno, Crete, 28-30 May 2015.

Daniel Gros, Brussels
Ansgar Belke, Essen

1. INTRODUCTION AND MOTIVATION

The euro area started as a pure 'monetary union'. It is now in the process of also becoming a 'banking union' (BU). EU leaders have argued that even this step is not enough. In September 2012, close to the peak of the euro crisis, a joint report by the four Presidents of the European Union (the Presidents of the European Commission, the European Council, the Eurogroup and the European Central Bank), entitled "Genuine Economic and Monetary Union", argued that much more was needed (Belke, 2013; Begg, 2014). The four Presidents argued in essence that the establishment of a banking union should also be seen as a first step towards further integration. According to their report, a fiscal union would be the next logical step. Moreover, a fiscal union was held to imply the need for a political union.

There is surprisingly little analytical support, however, for the claim that a banking union needs to lead to a fiscal union (Belke, 2013 and 2013a). The key argument most often heard is simply the observation that the euro area has only a very limited central budget (at least compared with other monetary unions), and that therefore there are almost no fiscal transfers to smooth asymmetric shocks. By contrast, the US, which is similar in size to the euro area, does have a substantial federal fiscal budget. The US experience is thus usually taken as a model of what is needed for a sustainable monetary union.

This study contributes to this debate by illustrating how the 'banking union' of the US provides very tangible insurance against local financial shocks, without major involvement of the 'fiscal union', which undoubtedly also exists in the US.[1]

The transatlantic financial crisis which started in 2007-08 and led to the Great Recession provides a key episode in assessing the importance of mechanisms to absorb regional shocks. The financial shocks quickly became regional in the euro area after 2009-10 when the financial systems of some countries almost collapsed and their sovereigns lost market access, e.g. Ireland, Portugal and Greece. It is often overlooked that the origins of the crisis in the US were also rather concentrated at the regional level. The housing boom was very concentrated in the US. The increase in housing prices varied enormously from state to state and only a few states (Arizona, Nevada, Florida and California) tended to account for most of the sub-prime lending, overbuilding and thus the subsequent economic distress and losses from delinquent mortgages.[2]

However, the US experienced 'only' a system-wide crisis in 2007-09. There was no specific crisis involving only those states where the real estate excesses had been most marked (Nevada, Florida and California). The main thrust of this study is that the US was better equipped to deal with these regional shocks because it is a fully fledged banking union.

The euro area officially has a banking union, but most observers would agree that it is incomplete if one starts with the three 'canonical' elements of a banking union (IMF, 2013a and b):

1) *Common supervision.* This has been achieved since the ECB, under the heading of the Single Supervisory Mechanism (SSM), has become the ultimate supervisor for all banks in the euro area, and the direct supervisor of about 130 of the

---

[1] For the debate on a "currency union with and without a banking union", see also the model-based contribution by Bignon, Breton and Breu (2013).

[2] This is not to deny that there was also a nation-wide element in the housing boom. Housing prices increased almost everywhere (and then fell almost everywhere). But the excesses (the "froth", in the words of Alan Greenspan) were concentrated in a few states.

largest banks accounting for about two-thirds of banking assets.

2)   *A common mechanism to resolve banks.* This has also been achieved with the creation of the Single Resolution Mechanism (SRM), which will be able to rely on a common fund, i.e. the Single Resolution Fund (SRF), after a transition period. The SRM will cover all banks in the euro area (and in those other EU countries wishing to join the SSM).

3)   *Common deposit insurance.* No agreement has been reached on this point. It remains to be seen how important this lacuna will become.

By contrast, the US has had all three elements in place at least since 1933.[3] The US thus qualifies as having had a banking union for over 80 years. (But one should also not forget that the US monetary union survived almost a century and a half without being a banking union.)

The central theme of this study is that the consequences of the US banking union could be seen during the financial crisis. A simple comparison of the fate of two different members of a large monetary union, after they were hit by a financial crisis, offers a powerful illustration of the importance of an integrated banking system. Ireland and Nevada, in fact, provide an almost ideal test case. These two entities share several important characteristics. For example, they both have similar populations as well as comparable GDP/GSP (gross domestic product/gross state product), and they both experienced an exceptionally strong housing boom. But when the boom turned to bust, the US states did not experience any local financial crisis (nor did any state government have to be bailed out).

---

[3] In that year, a common mechanism and fund for both deposit insurance and resolution was created in the form of the Federal Deposit Insurance Corporation. The FDIC was created after most of the 50 state-based deposit insurance schemes went bankrupt as a country-wide banking crisis led to the failure of hundreds of banks.

We find that the key difference between Nevada and Ireland is that banking problems in the US are handled at the federal level (the US is a banking union), whereas in the euro area, responsibility for banking losses remains national. Moreover, we also find that large banks with a wide footprint can also help to absorb regional shocks (at the cost of transmitting them to the entire system).

This book is organised as follows. The next chapter presents some case studies of the stabilisation properties of a banking union. Chapter 3 then analyses the role of 'foreign-owned banks' as a sort of 'private banking union'. Chapter 4 looks at the institutions that paid for the shock absorption provided by the official US federal banking-related institutions: the Federal Deposit Insurance Corporation (FDIC) and government-sponsored enterprises (GSEs), commonly known as Fannie Mae and Freddie Mac. Chapter 5 speculates on the extent to which European banking union as currently planned could provide comparably strong protection against regional shocks. Chapter 6 presents some considerations on the degree of financial integration in the euro area and discusses how the insurance premia within the SRM should be determined. Chapter 7 contains some general considerations with respect to a fiscal union and financial shock absorbers and the final chapter offers conclusions.

2. THE MACROECONOMIC STABILISATION PROPERTIES OF A BANKING UNION: SOME CASE STUDIES

In this chapter we analyse the implications of a banking union for macroeconomic stability by making comparisons between countries/states that have experienced similar local boom-bust cycles in real estate, but are part of different federal systems in terms of financial markets.[4]

The comparison pairs are Ireland-Nevada, Spain-Florida and Latvia-Nevada. The first two pairs are part of a larger currency area. The Latvia-Nevada comparison is interesting because Latvia was not in the euro area during its boom-bust cycle, but its banking system was dominated by banks from Nordic countries. In this sense, Latvia benefited from some protection provided within the 'Nordic Banking Union'.[5]

The pairing Ireland-Nevada is the one that comes closest to a natural experiment as these two entities are of a very similar size and had a very similar boom and bust in terms of real estate. The key difference, of course, is that the banks operating in

---

[4] The starting point for this section is Gros (2012b).

[5] At the time (2008), Latvia operated under a currency board arrangement and was hoping to adopt the euro soon. The tensions over the exchange rate of the Lat (although they were resisted in the end) seemed to create an illustration of the benefits of membership. And at that time, there were still relatively few tensions within the euro area, which thus appeared as a haven of stability. The Greek crisis erupted much later. The pay-off from a quick adjustment was thus stronger for Latvia than it was for Greece.

Nevada are part of the fully integrated and wider US banking system to such a degree that one cannot really speak of a 'banking system of Nevada'. The analysis will show that this was decisive for the limited impact of the great recession on the local economy and local public finances in Nevada (and other US states with similar local real estate booms).

Florida can similarly be compared to Spain. Both of these entities represent larger, more diversified economies than either Nevada or Ireland. Somewhat surprisingly (it was stated above that real estate booms tend to bear a regional character), real estate investments seem to have played a larger role in Spain, although the country is somewhat larger than Florida.

Another useful comparison is that between Nevada and Latvia or the other Baltic countries. None of the latter was part of the euro area when the crisis struck them in 2008-09, although they all had fixed their exchange rate to the euro and were thus informally in an (asymmetric) currency union with the euro area. Nevertheless, they weathered the crisis more quickly than Ireland, or other peripheral euro-area countries, because they benefited from the fact that their banks were largely owned by big Nordic banks which were able to absorb the losses that arose when the housing boom collapsed and the Baltic economies experienced a very sharp recession. It is interesting that the only Baltic country that needed a bailout was Latvia, which was also the only country that still had a significant local bank.

Before going more deeply into these comparisons, it is useful to consider the extent to which the boom-bust cycle is different between the US and the euro area at the aggregate level.

2.1 Regional concentration of real estate cycles within a monetary union

The aggregate data on housing prices and construction activity (as a percentage of GDP) reveals a considerable similarity. The boom was actually somewhat more pronounced in the US than in the euro area, at least if one looks at aggregate numbers. Housing prices increased by more in the US and then fell by more, but also recovered earlier, thus ending up at a similar level relative to that of the euro area (EA), if one looks at the period since the start of monetary union (Figure 1, right-hand side).

Figure 1. Development of the real estate sector – the US vs the euro area (1995-2012)

Construction (% of GDP)

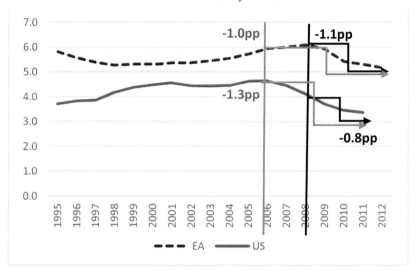

Housing prices (index 2000=100)

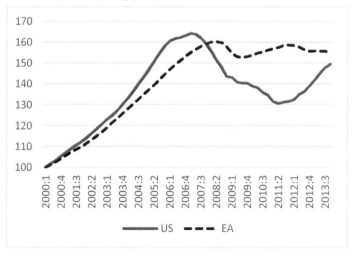

Data source: Eurostat.

An even more important indicator of the potential cost of a real estate cycle is the amount of construction activity undertaken (Figure 1, left-hand side). A large stock of unsellable houses often constitutes the main reason for losses on mortgages. Here again, one finds that the cycle was somewhat more pronounced in the US than in the euro area since construction spending fell by about 1.3 percentage points of GDP in the US, but only about 1.1 percentage points of GDP (on aggregate) in the euro area.

How could one then explain that the US recovered earlier from the bust of the housing bubble and that there were very serious difficulties at the national level in Europe, even in countries like Ireland or Spain, where public finance had been under control?

It is tempting to argue that the lack of regional problems in the US was due to a more uniform manifestation of the boom in the US than in the euro area. Within the euro area the average number hides fundamental differences between the peripheral countries Spain and Ireland, where both housing prices and construction activity boomed until 2007, and core countries like Germany where both housing prices and construction activity were relatively weak (again until 2007-08).

However, the boom-bust was also very concentrated in the US. Figure 2 below shows the distribution of the losses sustained by the Federal Deposit Insurance Corporation (FDIC) during the last crisis in each state. It is apparent that the banking problems were highly concentrated in a few states (small dots indicate losses above 3% of GSP, diagonal stripes 1.5-2% of GSP and solid filler, below 0.5% of GSP).

This combination of a similar boom/bust pattern in the aggregate variables and a similar degree of concentration at the regional level already suggests that the structure of the financial system and its backup mechanism must have played a key role in containing regional problems in the US.

Figure 2. Distribution of losses sustained by the FDIC from the 2007-08 sub-prime crisis (% of GSP)

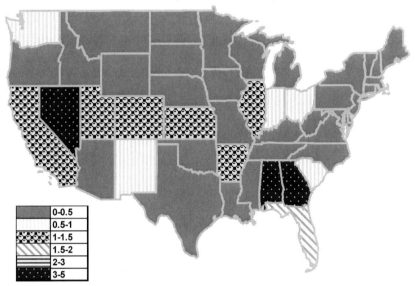

	0-0.5
	0.5-1
	1-1.5
	1.5-2
	2-3
	3-5

Source: Configured by the authors based on data from FDIC documents.

2.2   Ireland vs Nevada

Ireland and Nevada share several important characteristics, as reflected in Table 1 below. Their populations are not overly different (2.7 million vs. 4.5 million) and rather similar levels of GDP/gross state product (GSP) ($120 billion vs. $200 billion), at least as a share of the eurozone and US GDP, respectively. Both experienced a strong recession and a very similar level of unemployment. However, the fall in GDP and GSP, respectively, was much larger in Ireland than in Nevada. As will be argued below, this was due to the fact that the losses arising from the real estate bust in Nevada were to a large extent absorbed by the US federal financial system.

Table 1. Key statistics on Nevada vs Ireland

	Nevada	Ireland
Population (million, 2011)	2.7	4.5
GSP/GDP ($/€ billion, 2011)	120	200
Change in GSP/GDP (2007-10)	-5.3%	-17.6%
Average net migration rate since 'bust' (2008) as percentage of total population	0.32%	0.09%
Unemployment rate (2011)	13.5%	14.4%

Data sources: Eurostat, US Bureau of Economic Analysis and US Census Bureau.

The most important similarity is, however, that they both experienced an exceptionally strong housing boom – and bust. The similarity of the boom-bust cycle is shown in Figures 3a to 3d:

- 3a shows (nominal) GSP and GDP increased by a very similar proportion during the boom and then fell.

- 3b shows the evolution of housing prices, which increased until 2007-08 and then fell. This was the first fall in housing prices during peace time for the US.

- 3c shows construction activity as a percentage of GDP (for Ireland) and of GSP (gross state product for Nevada). It is again apparent that the two series follow the same pattern, but construction activity seems to have been much more important to the economy of Ireland than to that of Nevada. However, this difference might be due to a difference in definition of the aggregate 'construction' in the national accounts.

- 3d shows the consequences for the real economy in terms of the unemployment rate, which also follows a similar pattern.

Figure 3. The boom-bust cycle: Nevada vs Ireland

Figure 3a. Nominal GSP and GDP (index 2000= 100)

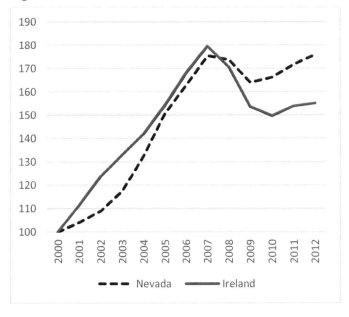

Figure 3b. Housing prices (2000=100)

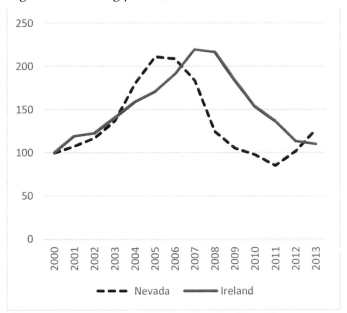

Figure 3c. Construction activity (% of GDP/GSP)

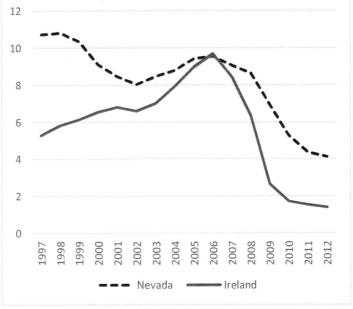

Figure 3d. Unemployment (% of the labour force)

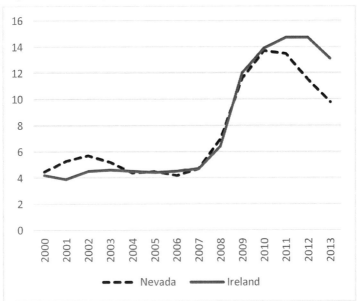

Data sources: Eurostat and US Bureau of Labour Statistics.

However, there is one fundamental difference between the two: when the boom turned to bust, Nevada did not experience any local financial crisis and the state government did not have to be bailed out. By contrast, the government of Ireland was for some time unable to issue any new debt on the market and had to be supported by a very large loan financed jointly by the IMF and the European rescue fund, i.e. the European Stability Mechanism (ESM) and its precursor, the European Financial Stability Facility (EFSF).

The key difference between Nevada and Ireland is that banking problems in the US are taken care of at the federal level (as the US is a banking union), whereas in the euro area, responsibility for banking losses was national, and will remain partially national until the SRF is fully operational.

Local banks in Nevada experienced huge losses (just like in Ireland) and many of them became insolvent, but this did not lead to any disruption of the local banking system as these banks were seized by the FDIC, which covered the losses and transferred the operations to other, stronger banks. In 2008-09, the FDIC thus closed 11 banks headquartered in the state, with assets of over $40 billion, or about 30% of GSP. The losses for the FDIC in these rescue/restructuring operations amounted to about $4 billion.[6]

---

[6] The initial loss estimates of the FDIC were later revised downwards to $2.4 billion, as some of the assets which the FDIC had to evaluate at crisis prices later recovered partially in value. However, the initial estimate constitutes the more important figure because it shows the amount of risk the FDIC was prepared to assume at the height of the crisis. During a financial crisis the perception of risk by the market and the ability to bear risk are more important than the exact amount of the losses that materialise once the crisis is over. The loss estimates of Fannie Mae and Freddie Mac were not revised as they represent just the sum of mortgages that did not perform. At first sight it appears that the loss rate for the FDIC was about 10%, not much higher than the 8% of bail-inable debt instruments that EU banks are supposed to hold under the regulations. This would seem to suggest that the likelihood that the SRM could face large losses should be minor. However, Washington Mutual (WaMu), which had its headquarters

Other losses were borne at the federal level when residents of Nevada defaulted in large numbers on their home mortgages. The two federal institutions that refinance mortgages have lost between them about $8 billion in the state since 2008.[7]

The federal institutions of the US banking union thus provided Nevada with a 'shock absorber' of about 8-9% of GSP, not in the form of loans, but in the form of an (ex-post) transfer because losses of this magnitude were borne at the federal level. (Against this transfer one would of course have to set the insurance premia paid by banks in Nevada prior to the bust. But they are likely to have been of a lesser magnitude.)

Of course, a lot of the banking business in Nevada was (and still is) conducted by 'foreign' banks, i.e. out-of-state banks, which just took the losses from their Nevada operations on their books and could set them against profits made elsewhere.[8] This is another way in which an integrated banking market can provide insurance against local financial shocks. One might call

---

in the state, represents a large part of the balance sheet of banks that were subject to intervention. However, given that there was no loss for the FDIC in this operation (WaMu was sold for $1), the loss rate on the other banks was much higher, about 30%.

[7] Fannie Mae and Freddie Mac have taken the unusual step of indicating their credit losses for those states hardest hit by the crisis (including Nevada, Florida and California, for example).

[8] The experience of WaMu constitutes a somewhat special case. The biggest bank to have failed in US history, a mortgage specialist, WaMu had its headquarters in Nevada (although the name suggests otherwise) and conducted some minor operations there. However, its failure did not lead to any local losses as WaMu was seized by the FDIC and its banking operations were sold for a very low sum to another large US bank (JP Morgan Chase) – but without any loss for the FDIC. Such an 'overnight' operation would have been impossible in Europe where no euro area-wide institution would have carried through a cross-border takeover of this size. Moreover, WaMu received about $80 billion in low-cost financing from the US Federal Home Loan Bank. Irish banks received massive amounts of low-cost emergency liquidity assistance from the ECB, but the Central Bank of Ireland had to guarantee these loans, which was not the case for the state of Nevada or for any bank in Nevada.

this a 'private' banking union (or a truly integrated banking market). It is impossible to estimate the size of this additional shock absorber, but the losses absorbed by out-of-state banks might very well have been at least as large again as the losses borne by the federal institutions. The total write-down of the large US banks, which operate across the entire US, was about $440 billion, twice as much as the $220 billion in losses of the three official institutions (FDIC, Fannie Mae and Freddie Mac). If these losses were distributed in a similar way to the losses of the official institutions mentioned so far, one could conclude that the shock absorption capacity of the large union-wide banks is likely to have been worth about 17% of GDP.

Nevada was also one of the states where 'non-conforming' or 'sub-prime' mortgages became particularly widespread. Non-conforming loans are not eligible for insurance and securitisation by the GSEs, but they were widely packaged into residential mortgage-backed securities (RMBS), which then were sold to investors worldwide. Some of these sub-prime securities remained on the balance sheets of the large US banks mentioned above. But a large part was bought by other US and foreign investors. These investors thus absorbed another part of the losses generated locally. The scale of this additional risk-sharing is very difficult to estimate precisely. But given that sub-prime issuance was also particularly widespread in Nevada it is likely that this risk-sharing was also substantial.

All in all, one can thus conclude that the overall loss absorption provided by the public institutions (FDIC and the two GSEs) and the private sector (large banks, sub-prime securitisation) must have been substantially larger than the 25.5% of GDP coming through the FDIC and the GSEs plus the banks (8.5% + 17% = 25.5%).

In Europe, there was no official risk-sharing in the sense that the Irish government had to take responsibility for saving the banks in Ireland. The ESM did provide financing for the Irish government when it lost market access. But the ESM could provide only loans, which have to be repaid with interest. Moreover, as an implicit condition of this support the Irish government was asked not to bail in investors holding the bonds of Irish banks.[9]

One consequence of this lack of risk-sharing was that public debt soared in Ireland. As shown in the Figure 4 below, just prior to the start of the crisis, Ireland had a very low debt/GDP ratio of around 25% of GDP, which was actually very similar to that of Nevada. The debt ratio of Nevada did not increase much, even though the housing cycle was very similar, as illustrated above. Today the debt ratio of Ireland is above 120% of GDP, six times that of Nevada.

Figure 4. Irish government debt vs the state of Nevada and local debt (% of GDP/GSP)

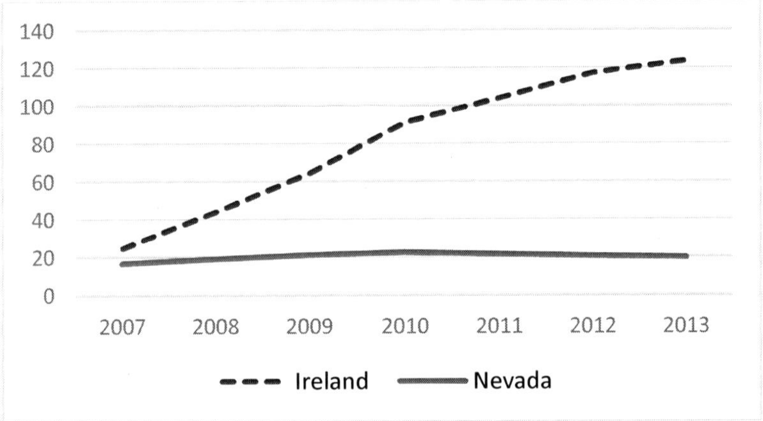

Source: Authors' own calculations.

[9] There has been considerable discussion about the importance of this bail-out of the bondholders, which often seems to be over-estimated. The legal framework was not totally clear on how to default on bond holders without going into a full bankruptcy. The amount at stake has been estimated at around €3-4 billion by the ECB. This is not an insignificant sum relative to the Irish economy (about 2% of GDP), but by itself would not have changed the outlook for Irish debt sustainability in a decisive way. Moreover, since part of the debt was held by Irish entities, including Irish pension funds, the burden of a 'private sector involvement' would have fallen in any event, at least partially, on Irish citizens. See McArdle (2012) for a comprehensive assessment of the matter.

In Europe, this 'private' banking union channel of risk mutualisation operates only in some cases. It is of paramount importance only for the smaller Baltic EU countries, whose banks are to a large extent in foreign hands. Estonia and Lithuania (and to a lesser extent Latvia) thus benefited before their entry into the euro area from similar protection against losses provided by the Scandinavian headquarters of their local banks. By contrast, most of the real estate lending in Ireland (and Spain) had mostly been extended by local banks so that most of the losses remained local (without any federal institution to provide insurance).[10]

The comparison between Nevada and Ireland thus clearly illustrates the shock-absorbing capacity of an integrated banking system and a banking union. For Nevada, the banking union resulted in a transfer worth over 25%, possibly up to 30%, of its income. Nevada is admittedly an extreme example of the housing boom and bust. Nevertheless, it illustrates the general point that a banking union can provide more shock-absorbing capacity than could ever be provided by any common budget ('fiscal capacity') that is currently being contemplated for the euro area.

2.3 Florida: Another example of the US banking union in action

Florida and Spain constitute another pair that can be used to illustrate the difference in the impact of a local real estate boom-bust cycle when there is a fully fledged banking union. Both Florida and Spain are much larger and more diversified economies than that of Ireland (or Nevada) and their housing cycles were less extreme. Table 2 below provides some of the basic data, showing that Florida is about half the size of Spain, both in terms of population and GSP, and that initially the impact

---

[10] It appears, however, that the larger UK banks, like RBS, also had substantial operations in Ireland, where they had to write off about £8 billion. Unfortunately, it is not possible to establish what proportion of the write-off resulted in actual losses and what part of any losses was incurred in the Republic of Ireland and what part in Northern Ireland.

on its GSP was very similar. However, the local labour markets reacted in a very different way.

Table 2. Key statistics on Spain vs Florida

	Spain	Florida
Population (millions, 2011)	46.1	19.1
Nominal GDP/GSP (€ billions, 2011)	1,063	542 ($770 billion)
Change in nominal GDP/GSP (2007-11)	1.0%	-0.9%
Unemployment rate (2011)	21.7%	10.5%
Change in unemployment rate (2007-11)	13.4pp	6.5pp

Source: Authors' own calculations.

Also, Figures 5a-d below provide an indication of the similarity in the cycle. Nominal GDP increased a bit more in Spain, but the downturn also lasted longer so that the increase in GDP was almost exactly the same over the entire cycle. A similar pattern can be seen for housing prices, which fell earlier in Florida, but then also started recently to recover; whereas Spanish housing prices continue to fall. Investment in construction follows exactly the same pattern, but has always been higher in Spain. It is in unemployment that one sees a decisive divergence with the bust. Unemployment rose initially in a similar way, but has continued to increase in Spain and has already declined substantially in Florida.

Figure 5. The boom-bust cycle in Florida vs Spain
Figure 5a. Nominal GSP/GDP (index 2000=100)

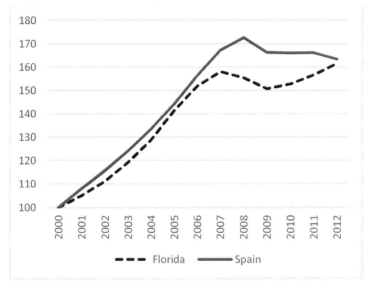

Figure 5b. Housing prices (index 2000=100)

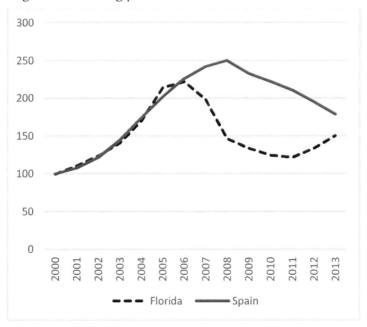

Figure 5c. Construction activity (% GDP/GSP)

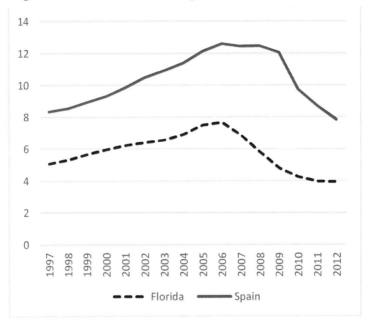

Figure 5d. Unemployment (% of labour force)

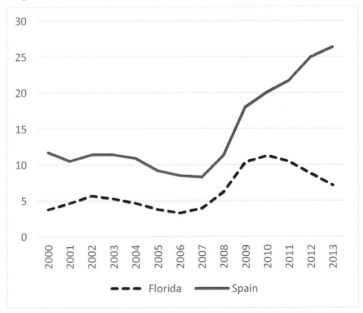

Data sources: Eurostat and US Bureau of Labor Statistics.

The key difference one has to explain is again that the state government of Florida was barely affected by the crisis whereas the government of Spain had to pay a substantial risk premium for issuing new debt. Moreover, when the full scale of the banking problems became apparent Spain received a loan of €60 billion (about 6% of its GDP) to help finance the recapitalisation of its problem banks (mainly the *cajas*, which had engaged in most of the real estate lending which caused most of the losses).

By contrast, in Florida one can see again the US banking union in action. During the period 2008-12 the FDIC closed over 70 banks headquartered in Florida, with total losses for the FDIC of roughly $14 billion, or 2% of Florida GSP.

Moreover, mortgages originating in Florida and covered by Fannie Mae and Freddie Mac experienced high default rates, leading to losses of the two GSEs of $19 billion since 2008. Federal loss-sharing on mortgages originating in Florida, but insured by the GSEs, thus amounted to another 2.3% of Florida's GSP. Total direct loss absorption through the official banking union amounted to about $33 billion, or 4.3% of GDP.

As argued above, one has to consider that in Florida (as in Nevada) the large US banks operating nationwide have a very large share. Under the maintained assumption that the losses at the large US banks operating nationwide were about twice those of the FDIC and GSEs combined, it follows that private sector losses borne 'out of state' might be twice as large as those assumed by the FDIC and GSEs, or probably another 8-9% of GDP.

The total loss absorption (ex post) of the private and public pillars of the US banking union for Florida was thus probably more than 12% of GSP. By comparison, Spain did receive a loan from the ESM, worth about 6% of its GDP, to help finance the recapitalisation of Spanish mortgage banks (*cajas*). But this was a loan and has to be repaid with interest.

As for Nevada, another form of loss absorption came through private sector securitisation. In the US, the most risky part (sub-prime) of the mortgages (which accounted for about

20% of all originations in Florida) were securitised and sold to capital market investors not only in the US, but also internationally (including many Europeans). Large US banks retained only part of the remaining risk. A further part of the local risk from sub-prime mortgages was thus borne by 'out-of-state' investors, protecting the economy of Florida, which could rebound earlier as its debt burden was much lighter.

2.4 Nevada vs Latvia

The Baltic states experienced strong growth rates in GDP and housing prices, and double-digit current account deficits until about 2007. This boom turned into a bust very quickly when global financial conditions worsened in 2007-08. The adjustment was then very sharp, with GDP falling by double-digit percentages as investment in construction virtually came to a standstill and credit dried up (Figures 6a-d).

Figure 6. The boom-bust cycle in Nevada vs Latvia

Figure 6a. Nominal GDP (index 2000=100)

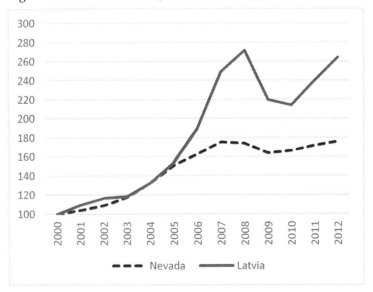

Figure 6b. Housing prices (index Nevada 2000=100 and Latvia 2006=100)

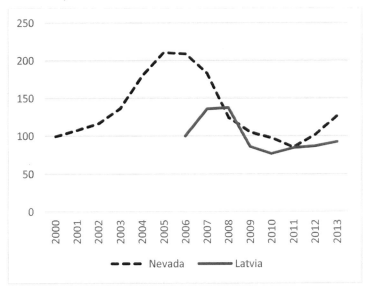

Figure 6c. Construction activity (% GSP/GDP)

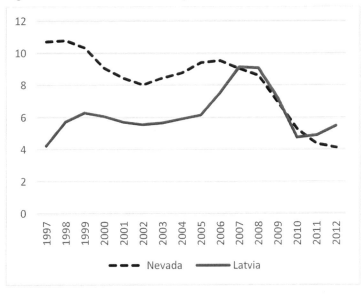

Figure 6d. Unemployment (% of work force)

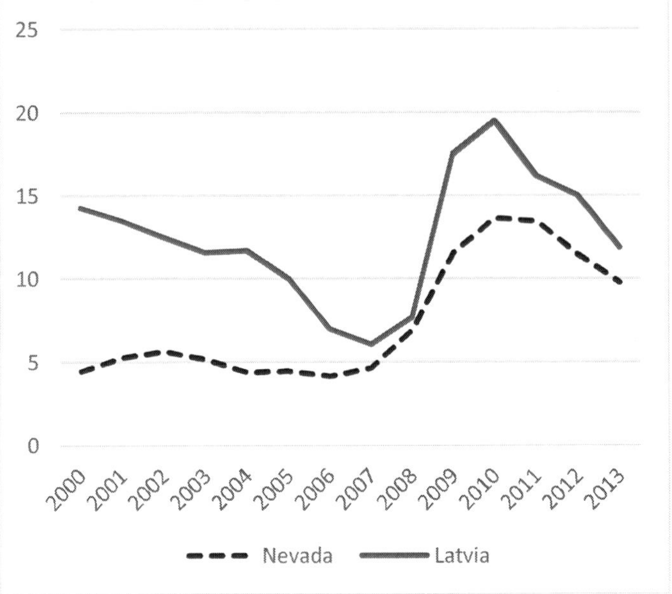

Data sources: Eurostat and US Bureau of Labor Statistics.

None of the Baltic countries was in the euro area when this occurred. This meant that their local banks could not access the various facilities of the ECB and the national central banks had to be rather restrictive, given that they wanted to defend their exchange rate against the euro. Only one of the Baltic countries, Latvia, needed international financial assistance, mainly to deal with the aftermath of the problems at its only large domestic bank.

Although Latvia was not then (2007-08) in the euro area, it still makes sense to compare it to Nevada because the adjustment patterns were similar due to the strong presence of foreign banks. Housing prices (available only since 2006) fell strongly when the crisis hit in 2008, but recovered already a few years later (as in Nevada) (Figure 6b). Unemployment first rose even more than in Nevada, but also started to improve after a few years, mimicking the pattern of Nevada (Figure 6d). In terms of construction activity, the upturn had been shorter and sharper in Latvia, but here also the recovery set in quickly (in contrast to

Nevada where the longer period of elevated construction activity probably led to a more significant housing overhang) (Figure 6c).

The one reason why this relatively early recovery was possible in Latvia (despite the fall in GDP of over 25%) was that foreign banks owned over 60% of the country's banking system. These banks thus absorbed most of the losses that arose when the Latvian housing market crashed in 2007-08.

Naturally, it is very difficult to pinpoint the origin of losses occurring within large internationally active banks. The available anecdotal evidence suggests that Swedish banks alone made loan losses in the Baltics of about $12-20 billion between 2009 and 2012, which would be several times greater than the capital invested in the local subsidiaries and would amount to between 15% and over 20% of the combined GDP of the three Baltic states.[11]

Given that other Scandinavian banks also had a significant part of the market in the Baltic states (about one-third, on average) it is thus likely that the total loss absorption by foreign banks in the Baltic states was closer to 30% of their GDP.

The Baltic states thus benefited enormously from the fact that their banking systems consisted essentially of subsidiaries of foreign banks. As loan losses were in many cases greater than the capital invested in these subsidiaries, the foreign (mostly Swedish) banks could have walked away from their daughter companies, which would have forced the Baltic governments to sustain them during the crisis. However, the Swedish (and other Nordic) banks chose to put additional capital into their Baltic subsidiaries because they were counting on the region's long-term growth potential.[12]

---

[11] See "Swedish banks can handle Baltic losses of 20 billion dollars" (www.baltic-course.com/eng/finances/?doc=14707; see also "Riksbank sees 2010 Baltic bank losses at USD 3.7 bln", (www.baltic-course.com/eng/finances/?doc=23185).

[12] See Ingves (2010) and "SEB banka has not yet recovered what it lost during financial crisis" (www.baltic-course.com/eng/finances/?doc=88286).

The broad conclusion that emerges is that one of the reasons why Latvia (as the other Baltic states) weathered the crisis more quickly than Ireland or Spain is that it benefited from the fact that its banks were to a large extent owned by larger Nordic banks, which were able to absorb the losses that arose when the housing boom collapsed and the Baltic economies experienced a very sharp recession. It is interesting to note that the only Baltic country that needed a bail-out was Latvia, which was also the only country that still had a significant local bank.

3. FOREIGN-OWNED BANKS: A BANKING UNION SUBSTITUTE? THE EU EXPERIENCE

The case studies presented in the previous chapter suggest that the large banks that operate throughout the entire US provided a very important channel through which local shocks could be better absorbed. The estimates provided above suggest that the shock-absorbing contribution from internationally active banks could have been twice as significant as the one provided by the official 'banking union' institutions (the FDIC and the GSEs). But cross-border banking has remained limited in Europe. Somewhat surprisingly, however, transnationally operating banks have played a more important role outside the euro area than within the euro area.

For example, Spain did not have protection from a banking union as there was little activity of foreign-owned banks in Spain. Moreover, most of the real estate-related lending that later caused most of the losses was done by the local *cajas* that financed their loan books not with local savings, but by attracting large inflows of foreign capital, mostly in the form of covered bonds or interbank loans, neither of which is loss-absorbing.

In the case of Ireland some loss absorption occurred because the large UK banks had a substantial exposure to Ireland and thus also absorbed some losses that occurred there, though the amounts are difficult to ascertain.

Against the original expectation that borders would no longer matter within a common currency area, there has been little cross-border integration of the banking sector within the euro area. But much more has occurred within the EU with large banks from the older member states taking over most of the banking systems in the new member states (west-east). This take-over of the local banking system was driven by the fact that the knowledge of how to run a bank had disappeared in the decades under the socialist system. The penetration of foreign banks was particularly strong in the small Baltic states, where Nordic banks had a market share of 80-90%. These banks had made large profits during the boom years, but then experienced large losses when the credit and real estate boom in the region ended abruptly in 2008-09, (Buch, Körner & Weigert, 2013: 9). Foreign banks thus absorbed most of the losses that occurred with the busts in Estonia, Latvia and Lithuania. It is interesting to note that the only exception to the dominance of foreign banks occurred in Latvia, where one significant local bank remained, but its problems almost pushed the government into insolvency.

The experience of the Baltic states shows that integration via equity markets (ownership) can mimic the shock-absorbing properties of a banking union: foreign-owned banks can absorb losses. However, this mechanism works only if the (until now national) supervisor allows them to maintain exposure. This willingness of the Swedish (and other Nordic) supervisors to allow their banks to maintain their exposure in the Baltic states and to recapitalise their subsidiaries there was a crucial element in stabilising the financial sector in the region.

Another condition for loss absorption by 'foreign banks' to be stabilising is that the foreign-owned banks must be strong enough to carry substantial losses. This condition was fulfilled since the Swedish and other banks that had large exposures in the Baltic states were able to absorb substantial losses, given that the business in their home base remained solid and given that their home economies were running large current account surpluses, which effectively insulated them from the flight of cross-border capital which started in 2010-11 when the broader financial crisis became the euro crisis.

The European experience has also shown that a strong presence of foreign banks can lead to a propagation of financial shocks abroad to the domestic economy. This happened during the first leg of the financial crisis when the large banks from the older member states came under funding stress and started to pull back capital and credit lines from their subsidiaries in Central and Eastern Europe. These banks came from countries like Italy, Austria or Belgium, whose fiscal and balance of payments position was weaker than those of the Scandinavian countries (like Sweden) whose banks dominated the Baltic banking market. This pullback by the foreign parents contributed to the economic downturn throughout Central and Eastern Europe, and threatened to initiate a self-reinforcing spiral of a withdrawal of financial support from the foreign parents, a deeper recession and therefore more local losses, prompting the foreign parents to accelerate their withdrawal. Moreover, each individual parent bank initially acted in isolation, hoping that the economic impact of its withdrawal would be limited since other banks could at least in principle take its place in financing the local economy.

It took an international initiative, coordinated by the international financial institutions, to bring the handful of key parent banks from Western Europe together. Under this so-called 'Vienna Initiative', the banks promised not to reduce their exposure to Central and Eastern European countries and the IMF agreed to provide the countries with substantial balance-of-payments support. This combination was sufficient to arrest the vicious circle described above since it helped to stabilise the economies in the region. This result, in turn, limited the losses for the parent banks, thus also providing a justification for the banks to continue to provide financing in the region.

This episode illustrates the general economic principle that 'there is no free lunch'. Large cross-border or cross-regional banks can mitigate the local impact of local financial shocks, but they also propagate shocks to the overall financial system to all regions in which they play an important role.

To return to the US example, one could thus argue that the presence of the large US banks throughout the US provided a shock-absorbing mechanism for Nevada or Florida, but also a shock-propagating mechanism for the northern states which did not experience a real estate boom. The financial crisis, which started when the sub-prime boom burst, led to a tightening of credit availability throughout the US, although the boom had been rather concentrated in a few states, as documented above.

4. WHO PAYS FOR THE SHOCK ABSORBERS?

One key issue for any shock-absorber mechanism is whether the mechanism is self-financing or needs public funding. This issue has played a key role in the political debate, both in the US and in the EU. The political slogan has been that 'the industry' should pay for its own mistake, and that 'taxpayer money' should not be used to bail out banks. These principles were at the basis of the construction of the Single Resolution Mechanism (SRM) and its Single Resolution Fund (SRF), which will be financed by contributions from industry. The size of the SRF could be kept relatively small because another piece of EU legislation, namely the Bank Resolution and Recovery Directive (BRRD), established tough rules on the 'bail-in' of creditors before a bank can receive financial support from the SRF. Ex ante, there is thus a clear intention to make the key pillar of the banking union in the eurozone self-financing, obviating the need for financial support from the budgets of member states.

It is of course too early to say whether the European banking union will be 'self-financing'.

In the US there are two 'official' shock-absorber mechanisms (the FDIC and securitisation by the GSEs), which have been operating for long enough to measure whether, ex post, the system did finance itself, i.e. whether the costs that had to be sustained were on average borne by the industry.

Since these two systems are of a different nature, they have to be discussed separately.

4.1 FDIC

Historically, the losses of the FDIC have come in two waves: the savings and loan (S&L) crisis of the 1980s and 1990s and the 'subprime' crisis of the last decade.

The losses the FDIC had to sustain after 2008 were greater than the fund it had accumulated during the previous boom years. At the start of the crisis, the FDIC had slightly over $50 billion at its disposal, equivalent to about 1.2% of insured deposits. However, already about one year into the crisis, the available funding was about to run out.

This is why the FDIC had to be supported by a large line of credit from the Treasury. The FDIC fund thus went negative to about $21 billion already in 2009-10, but it was replenished quickly because the FDIC was able to force banks to pre-pay assessments up to 2012, bringing the fund quickly back into the black. However, it will take another decade or so before the FDIC will again reach its target level of 1.25% of insured deposits.[13]

The FDIC's funding will thus be reconstituted by contributions from industry. This part of the US banking union thus needed liquidity support from the federal institutions during the biggest financial crisis in living memory. But in the end, the FDIC remained solvent.

By contrast, a large part of the S&L crisis in the 1980s and 1990s was ultimately borne by the federal budget.

The S&L crisis was different.[14] Over 1,000 so-called 'thrifts' were closed or otherwise subjected to intervention (of the 3,000 that had existed before the crisis).[15]

---

[13] For more detailed information see "FDIC Statistics at a glance" (www.fdic.gov/bank/statistical/stats/2012mar/fdic.html).

[14] For a description of the savings and loan crisis in the US, see https://en.wikipedia.org/wiki/Savings_and_loan_crisis.

[15] A thrift is a financial institution focusing on taking deposits and originating home mortgages. Thrift banks often have access to low-cost

In this case the government was needed not for liquidity, but to bail out the institutions that were in principle responsible for insuring deposits at these institutions (the S&Ls had a separate deposit guarantee system). At the time the FDIC was not responsible for the 'thrifts' whose deposit guarantee system was organised separately on a sectoral basis. As the sector was much weakened after the crisis (and given that the losses were great relative to the size of the sector), it was not possible to recover the cost from the surviving institutions later. The total losses for US taxpayers amounted to about $130 billion or about 1% of US GDP at the time.

The S&L crisis was also different in that it involved large-scale fraud and was not related to a system-wide weakness in other segments of the financial market. However, the S&L crisis was regionally very concentrated, with a few states, in particular Texas, accounting for most losses, as can be seen in Figure 7 below in which states with zero losses are shown in solid filler and vertical lines, and those with losses above 3% are indicated by small dots, horizontal lines and circles. In this case again, however, there were no spillover effects for the budgets of Texas or the other states in which the S&L crisis was concentrated because the losses were first absorbed by the S&L safety net, which was organised on a nationwide basis. When that proved insufficient, the federal government assumed the remaining losses in order to make depositors whole. The losses assumed at the federal level amounted to over 10% of the GSP of Texas at the time.

---

funding from Federal Home Loan Banks, which allows for higher savings account yields to customers and increased liquidity for mortgage loans. It is also known as a "savings and loan association".

Figure 7. Distribution of the losses from the S&L crisis sustained by FDIC and precursors (% of GSP)

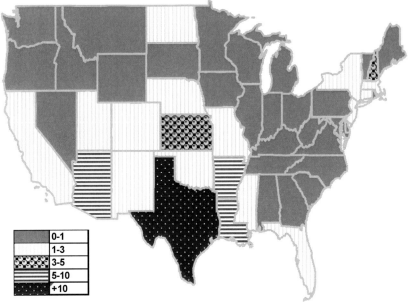

	0-1
	1-3
	3-5
	5-10
	+10

Source: Authors' own configuration based on data from FDIC documents.

As an aside, one should note the important role of commercial real estate loans played during the S&L crisis. Commercial real estate is potentially riskier because the borrower is a limited liability company, thus the recovery value rests only on the value of the land and its buildings. In the case of single family mortgages, by contrast, the debtor remains in principle liable for the entire amount of the loan, even if the value of the is lower (deficiency payments). This is the case in at least some states in the US. An historical report by the FDIC on the S&L crisis concluded:

> … in 1980, banks that subsequently failed had 43 percent of their total real estate loan portfolio in commercial real estate loans; by 1993 this had increased to about 69 percent. In contrast, non-failed banks were more conservatively invested: in 1980, 32 percent of their total real estate loan portfolio was invested in

commercial real estate loans, and by 1993 the percentage was still approximately the same.[16]

4.2 Securitisation via US federal housing-market institutions

The two GSEs package 'conforming mortgages', i.e. mortgages conforming to certain stringent criteria that ensure a very high probability of repayment, and sell them to investors as so-called mortgage backed securities (MBS). However, the securities issued by the GSEs are de facto ultimately guaranteed by the US federal government because the GSEs securitise only mortgages that have been insured by them or another federal housing finance institution. In principle, there should thus not be any losses for investors on any mortgage that enters into an MBS issued by the two GSEs. When a mortgage that is packaged and securitised by either of the GSEs goes into default, the loss is made good by the insurance arm of the GSE. This implies that the shareholders of the GSEs ultimately had to bear any losses when many households could not or did not want to service their mortgages. When the losses mounted, the federal government had to put additional capital into the GSEs; it thus appeared that the losses would have to be borne by the taxpayer.

The losses of the GSEs on their mortgages were in general limited since they accepted only 'conforming' mortgages, i.e. those with sufficient documentation, proof of income, a fixed interest rate and a loan-to-value ratio typically at most 80%.

However, during the boom years (2003-07), a large proportion of mortgages were non-conforming, most of them euphemistically called 'sub-prime' because they were lacking proper documentation, had 'teaser' rates (instead of the US standard of 30 years fixed) and were for a higher proportion of the value of the house than accepted by the GSEs (going in some cases above 100%). These 'non-conforming' mortgages were not eligible for securitisation by the two GSEs and were sold as so-

---

[16] See chapter 3, "An Examination of the Banking Crises of the 1980s and early 1990s" in FDIC (1997, pp 137-165).

called 'private label' MBS (mortgage-backed securities) (see next section).

There is little sign of a link between sub-prime origination and losses for the federal institutions. Indeed, it is a priori uncertain whether higher private (sub-prime) and higher 'conforming' mortgage lending should go hand in hand: rising housing prices make sub-prime loans appear to be a safe bet, thus leading to higher sub-prime origination overall. But given housing prices (and building activity), a higher proportion of sub-prime origination should mean lower losses for the FDIC and the GSEs, as more of the risk is borne by the private sector.

The GSEs had never experienced any overall losses before the 'sub-prime' crisis. This was because during normal times the loss rates on the 'conforming' mortgages that the GSEs insure and securitise are rather low and the insurance premia the GSEs were charging were, on average, sufficient to cover these small loss rates. Of course, the loss rates declined even further during the housing boom with its soaring housing prices of the early 2000s. With rising housing prices, the value of the collateral increased. Even if the homeowner could not service the mortgage, the GSEs, which had kept loan-to-value (LTV) ratios below 80%, were unlikely to make a loss when the underlying mortgage went into delinquency and the house (GSEs typically insure mortgages on single-family homes) had to be sold. However, this changed when housing prices started to fall in the wake of the financial crisis and unemployment soared. Widespread unemployment put many families in difficulty and the lower housing prices meant that foreclosure more often resulted in a loss.

During the early years of the crisis, the GSEs thus suffered great losses, as documented above. These losses were greater than the capital they had. The government thus had to step in and refinance them. However, the losses incurred in the period 2008-12 are now in the process of being made up, as the insurance premia have increased and delinquency rates are falling. This part of the US banking union is thus likely to become self-financing.

To put it in another way: the insurance against regional shocks provided de facto by the GSEs has in the end been financed entirely by investors (and mortgage holders). One key reason why the losses of the GSEs have now been made up is that only a very small proportion (6%) of the newer loans has a mark-to-market LTV ratio above 100%, whereas that proportion was 40% during the boom years 2005-08, as shown in the second to last column of the table below. It is thus not surprising that the delinquency ratio rose to almost 10% on the mortgages from the boom years, but is now only 0.35% for newer mortgages.

Table 3. Selected credit characteristics of single-family conventional loans, by acquisition period (% of total)

	As of 31 March 2013			
	Single-family conventional guarantee book of business	Current estimated mark-to-market LTV ratio	Current mark-to-market LTV ratio >100%	Serious delinquency ratio
New single-family book of business	69%	70%	6%	0.35%
Legacy book of business				
2005-08	20%	96%	40%	9.77%
2004 and prior	11%	56%	6%	3.57%
Total single-family book of business	100%	74%	13%	3.02%

Data source: Fannie Mae, Quarterly Report for the period ending 31 March 2013, submitted to the US Securities and Exchange Commission, p. 5 (www.fanniemae.com/resources/file/ir/pdf/quarterly-annual-results/2013/q12013.pdf).

4.3   Other (private label) securitisation

During the credit boom many households were able to obtain mortgages even if the payment record and the credit score of the mortgage holder was below the minimum required by the GSEs or with an LTV ratio above the 80% permitted by Fannie Mae and Freddie Mac. These mortgages, which were not 'conforming' to the standards of the GSE, were euphemistically called 'sub-prime' and packed in securities called residential mortgage-backed securities (RMBS) and sold in different tranches, many of which were rated AAA because during the boom years housing prices were increasing and the loss rates on these loans were low. The AAA-rated tranches were sold to investors worldwide as they were considered a safe investment given the expectation that housing prices would continue to increase.

This form of securitisation provided another important element of regional shock absorption because during the bust the default and delinquency rates on these mortgages rose even more than the conforming mortgages, which had been insured by the GSE (and the losses as a percent of the mortgage were higher). These private-label MBS were different from the covered bonds, which are widely used in Europe, in that the principal of the various tranches was not guaranteed. This system of risk distribution thus did not involve any public expenditure.

The losses that arose in particular in those states where sub-prime lending had been most prevalent, e.g. Nevada and Florida, were thus not borne by the local banks in these states, but rather by the ultimate investors in the RMBS, many of which were banks from countries with excess savings, like Germany. Unfortunately, it is difficult to document the loss absorption through this channel as there are no reliable statistics on the ultimate holders of the different private-label MBS.

This is, of course, an ex-post view. One could also argue that the possibility to securitise sub-prime mortgages led to serious moral hazard problems as the originating banks and brokers had an incentive to originate as much business as possible without taking into account the ability of the borrower to service the mortgage since the risk of default would be borne by the holders of the RMBS.

4.4 Who pays in the end? The incidence of taxes in a competitive industry

No taxpayer money was thus spent to support the official shock-absorbing institutions of the US after the sub-prime crisis. In this sense the US provides a model of how to reach the often stated aim of having 'industry' pay for the cost of a financial crisis.

However, the losses of the FDIC and the GSEs had to be borne by somebody. This collective somebody were financial sector shareholders and clients. The GSEs had little equity, thus most of the losses from the excess lending during the boom years had to be compensated by higher-risk premia paid by families who took their mortgage during the bust. Similarly, FDIC losses have to be compensated by new levies on bank deposits. General theorems of public finance imply that the cost of these additional levies will be 'translated' to customers in the form of lower returns on deposits or higher interest rates if banking is a competitive business.

This is the basic conundrum facing those who hold that 'the industry' should pay for its own mistakes because taxpayer money should not be used to shore up failing banks. Ex ante, capital flows into the industry up to the point at which it can be expected to earn a normal, risk-adjusted return. This implies that the cost of contributing to future bank rescues will be factored in by investors as an element in their decisions, leading them to demand higher-risk premia. This means that industry customers will ultimately bear the expected cost of future rescues in the form of lower deposit rates, higher lending rates or generally higher fees for banking services. The capital cushions accumulated by the higher-risk premia during tranquil times will then be needed when a crisis arises. Ex post, industry capital can then be used to pay for the cost of any rescues and it might thus appear that 'the industry paid for its own mistake'. Ex ante, this is impossible to ensure in a competitive environment.

5. WHAT TO EXPECT FROM THE EUROPEAN BANKING UNION?

The key aim of the banking union was to break the 'diabolic feedback loop' between banks and sovereigns.[17] With the legislative framework now in place, one could ask how regional instability would be dealt with under such a union.

To illustrate the importance of the banking union, one needs only to perform the thought experiment of how the boom-bust cycle in Ireland would have played out with the Single Resolution Fund (SRF) fully in operation, i.e. after the end of the transition period.[18]

The most visible difference would of course arise during the downturn since the local banks would naturally run into difficulties as the local real estate boom turns to bust. If the Irish real estate bust had occurred under the banking union the consequences for the Irish government would have been quite different from what happened in 2008, 2009 and 2010 when the Irish government first felt obliged to give a blanket guarantee for all liabilities of its banks and then was prevented from bailing in the few instruments which were not covered by the guarantee.

---

[17] In this context, Allard et al. (2013) emphasise that the inability to cope with shocks is a systemic problem, i.e. not just for the affected country, but also for others due to the rapid spillover of fiscal stress.

[18] Formally, it will take 10 years for the SRF to reach its target of €55 billion and the full merger of the national 'compartments' within the SRF will be achieved after eight years. This might appear a rather long transition, but the mutualisation will proceed relatively quickly at the beginning since 60% of national compartments within the SRF will be merged after only two years. The gradual increase in the degree of mutualisation agreed corresponds to the proposal made by Gros & Schoenmaker (2012).

With the banking union in place, the funding for keeping Irish banks alive would have come from the SRF. The Irish government would have sustained losses only if the SRF had decided not to save the local banks and the losses had been so great that the national deposit insurance scheme would have had to intervene to ensure that no holder of an insured retail deposit made a loss.

In the case of another Ireland-type real estate boom and bust the ECB would signal the banks in difficulty to the SRF, which would then decide whether to allow some banks to fail, put them into resolution or save them because they are judged systemic. The funds needed to save any banks (or enable an orderly resolution) would come from the SRF, not from the national government, as is the case today.

The 'diabolical' feedback loop between weak banks and weak sovereigns, which was so destructive at the height of the euro crisis, should thus be broken from the start (Belke, 2014; Begg, 2014).

Moreover, the banking union might also have limited the size of the booms and the size of the exposure of the national banking system to its real estate sector. National supervisors had a natural tendency to protect the independence of 'their' banks, thus limiting de facto in many cases cross-border mergers and acquisition and the formation of multinational banks. Cross-border equity investment in the banking sector should now become more frequent, which constitutes a further stabilising factor as the experience of the Baltic countries has shown.

In future a national real estate boom-bust cycle is thus likely to play out very differently. A future Ireland-type bust is less likely to entail severe distress for the sovereign. This does not mean that the Nevada scenario of no stress at all for the local sovereign would materialise, given that the other elements of the US banking union (securitisation via the GSEs, federal deposit insurance and large banks which operate throughout the area) are missing in Europe. But the extreme stress on sovereigns observed in the cases of Ireland and Spain should become much less likely.

Moreover, it is likely that the European institutions, not only the SSM but also the European Systemic Risk Board (ESRB), would have recognised the existence of a regional housing price boom, and would have been much more likely than a local supervisor to warn banks about excessive real estate valuations, thus limiting the extent of over-lending and construction.

The potential losses for the SRF would anyway probably be lower than those incurred by the Irish government because of the bail-in rules under the BRRD, which mandates that public funds can be provided if not only shareholders but also some creditors have accepted a loss (have been 'bailed in') of 8% of the bank's assets. This did not happen in the case of Ireland because at that time the entire euro area banking system was in difficulty, and because it was thought that letting any Irish banks fail would have sparked another panic, comparable to the one that followed the failure of Lehman Brothers in the autumn of 2008.

For banks subject to intervention by the SRF, it would of course become relevant whether the debt instruments that are bailed in are held predominantly by residents, local households or other local financial intermediaries. If other local financial institutions are heavily invested in the 'bail in-able' instruments of local banks an important channel would still remain for local contagion. This was up to now the case, as until 2008 a large part of cross-border investment within the euro area was in the most secure or short-term spectrum, such as short-term interbank deposits and covered bonds. By contrast, hybrid forms of capital, which would be the first to be bailed in, have been until now sold locally in Europe. One reason is that often these instruments are tailor-made to be tax efficient under the local legal system. Another reason is that the information needed to evaluate hybrid capital is also available mostly in the home country.

In the specific case of Ireland a large part of the real estate lending had been financed by interbank deposits from other countries; and these deposits were mostly of a maturity longer than seven days, and could thus have been bailed in under the new rules contained in the BRRD. If the BRRD had been in force the Irish crisis might have taken a different course. But it remains to be seen whether interbank deposits (with a maturity longer than seven days) will again become as important as they were until 2007-08.

Another potential channel of contagion from banks to the sovereign arises from Article 109 of the BRRD which stipulates that the (national) deposit guarantee scheme (DGS) has to contribute to the funding of resolution to the extent of the losses the DGS would have faced if the bank in question had been left go bankrupt. This makes sense from the point of view of protecting the funds of the SRF, but it opens a Pandora's box of practical issues. First of all, it is always very difficult to estimate the losses the opening of a bankruptcy procedure would produce. This could also be observed in the cases of the two major bankruptcies which happened during the 2008 crisis, namely Lehman Brothers and the Icelandic banks. Immediately after the insolvency proceedings were opened, the price of the unsecured bonds of these institutions fell drastically, sometimes to as little as less than 10% of their face value. However, the prices of these bonds rose strongly later as the insolvency proceedings advanced and it became clearer that the assets were worth more than had been thought originally (partially this was due to the general recovery of asset values which set in in 2009). Moreover, for any international bank or banking group it will be even more difficult to determine in which subsidiary of the group the losses are to be located. There are thus likely to be strong conflicts of interest among the national DGSs which insure the deposits of the subsidiaries in different countries.

These valuation problems are particularly acute given that the decision on the bail-in and the involvement of the SRM will typically have to be taken over the course of a weekend. Fortunately, paragraph 5 of Article 109 BRRD limits the contribution of the DGS to one-half of the target level of funds the DGS in question contains. The target level of the funds for a DGS is typically less than 1% of GDP. The maximum contribution the SRF can demand from any one DGS is thus less than one-half of 1% of GDP.

The local contagion might of course be even stronger if the SRM lets some banks fail, i.e. if the SRF does not intervene. In this case the local DGS would have to bear at least part of the burden (provided the losses are larger than the bail-inable capital of 8% of assets). Moreover, when the losses are very large relative to the balance sheet of the bank(s) involved there is no limit to the size of the losses the DGS might have to cover. In the case of large international banking groups national DGSs might experience quite different loss rates. This constitutes another aspect of the conflicts of interest between the SRF and the (national) DGS, because a high contribution by the SRF to keep the bank in question afloat would mean a lower risk of losses for the DGS. Representatives of the SRF might thus argue that the local DGS should contribute to any rescue operation, although the latter has no legal obligation to do so as long as the bank is not formally insolvent.

All in all, one can conclude the (incomplete) banking union created for the euro area is likely to diminish the strength of the feedback loop from weak banks to their national sovereign. However, large banks with very large losses could still create problems for their national government.

6. OPEN ISSUES FOR BANKING UNION

This chapter deals with some of the open issues that remain if the banking union is to become a bulwark against regional financial shocks. The purpose is not to be exhaustive, but to briefly discuss some of the major issues that remain. Two short-term issues are the lack of a fiscal backstop for the Single Resolution Fund (SRF) and its financing via risk-related contributions. A third issue concerns the lack of an agreement on a common deposit insurance scheme. Official decisions have recently been taken in both areas, but they appear to lack ambition.[19]

The main financial element of the banking union will be the SRF. This fund will be created together with the Single Resolution Mechanism (SRM) via a separate Intergovernmental Agreement (IGA) and not via the normal procedure based on the EU Treaty. However, this legal particularity should not impair the proper functioning of the SRM as a 'federal' institution.

Officially, the purpose of the SRF is not to absorb losses but only to provide temporary financing for banks that need to be restructured (Belke, 2014). Reality might be quite different, given that any policy on bank resolution suffers from acute time inconsistency: during tranquil times it is in the interest of the public authorities to announce that they do not intend to bail out

---

[19] The agreement on the contributions to the SRF can be found at http://ec.europa.eu/internal_market/finances/banking-union/single-resolution-mechanism/index_en.htm. The agreement on DGS can be found at http://ec.europa.eu/internal_market/bank/guarantee/index_en.htm.

the creditors of any bank, hoping that this will make the creditors of banks aware of the risk they are running.

When a bank experiences difficulties, however, there is always an extremely strong temptation to bail out either the bank itself or its creditors. The reason is that the insolvency of a bank can trigger extremely serious contagion effects and endanger systemic stability, as the default of Lehman Brothers clearly showed. However, this problem is not specific to the SRM; it affects all resolution funds when dealing with a potentially systemic crisis.[20]

However, there remain two questions that are pertinent to the financing of the SRM.

6.1 Can the SRF survive without a fiscal backstop?

The size of the SRF has often been criticised as being underfunded. But this is largely mistaken. A fund of €55 billion would be sufficient to resolve all but the very largest banks in Europe (based on the rule of thumb that the cost of resolution usually does not exceed a small multiple of own funds). It would also be sufficient to deal with even a systemic crisis in small- to medium-sized countries (Spain needed €60 billion from the ESM).

Moreover, the EU (draft) Regulation establishing the SRM specifies also that the SRF can, if needed, raise ex-post levies. For any given year the limit for the ex-post levies is three times the 'normal' annual contributions, or 3 x 12.5 = 37.5% of the total (target) fund, or about €20 billion. Over time these ex-post levies could provide the SRF with important additional funding.

The SRM is of course relatively small compared to the overall assets of the SSM banking system (which amount to over €25 trillion) and also small relative to the overall capital of the sector (about €1 trillion). But one cannot expect a resolution fund

[20] See for example Acharya & Yorulmazer (2007), who stress the problem of 'too many to fail'. Chari & Kehoe (2009) analyse the link with optimal regulation. Other contributions in this vein are Gimber (2012) and Grochulsky (2011).

to deal with the chronic under-capitalisation of the European banking sector (see also Beck, Gros & Schoenmaker, 2013). The resources of the SRF will be significant relative to the capitalisation of most individual banks (the 30 German banks directly under the SSM have on average capitalisation of only €10 billion). Moreover, the resources of the SRF will loom large relative to the budget of any single member state, except the largest ones.

Any restructuring fund can only be a first-aid kit for a small number of occasional accidents. A systemic crisis always requires a fiscal backstop. The euro area at present does not have such an explicit backstop in that it is not clear who would lend to the SRF should its funds not be sufficient to deal with a crisis which is systemic at the level of the euro area. (As argued above, the SRF should be able to deal with a systemic crisis in any small to medium-sized member country.)

One can argue, however, that an implicit backstop exists, as experience has shown that during a crisis, when there was a need for public funds, they were found. The process was of course slow and cumbersome and the sluggish creation of the ESM made the crisis even worse. But there is now agreement that a (small) part of the resources of the ESM would be available for a direct recapitalisation of banks if a member country is not able to raise the funds on its own.[21]

Moreover, if the resources committed for bank recapitalisation by the ESM should prove to be insufficient, it would take only a further political decision to provide a backstop to the SRF in the event of a truly systemic crisis. This choice will be politically natural once the ESM's lending capacity of €700 billion has been restored, which should be the case once the current programmes have ended and the funds have been reimbursed. It is clear that it would be preferable to have an explicit, Treaty-based, backstop for the SRF. A legal guarantee

---

[21] For the official decision, see www.consilium.europa.eu/uedocs/cms_data/docs/pressdata/en/ecofin/137569.pdf.

does not seem to be indispensable, however, since it seems that even in the US the backing of the Treasury for the FDIC is based on a political decision taken a long time ago, rather than being mandated by law.[22]

6.2 How to discourage risk-taking via the contributions to the SRF

There is general agreement that the banking sector should pay for its own safety net. Resolution and deposit guarantee funds should thus be financed by contributions from the banks themselves. This principle is at the basis of the approach taken in the EU Directive on (national) DGSs that has recently been passed. And it is also enshrined in the basic rules of the SRF, which will be at the disposal of the SRM that has also been recently approved (see Article 69 of the SRM Regulation).

Moreover, there is also general agreement that the contributions individual banks pay to the resolution (or deposit guarantee) fund should be based on the riskiness of the bank itself. This is essential to providing individual banks with the proper incentives.

However, in reality a practical problem arises: resolution or deposit guarantee funds (whether national DGS or the SRF) also have a target level, usually as a percentage of deposits or some other liability. Once this target level has been reached,

---

[22] On the issue of the 'full faith and credit' backing for the FDIC, one finds the following explanation: In light of apparent systemic risks facing the banking system, the adequacy of FDIC's financial backing has come into question. Beyond the funds in the Deposit Insurance Fund above and the FDIC's power to charge insurance premia, FDIC insurance is additionally assured by the federal government (see http://en.wikipedia.org/wiki/Federal_Deposit_Insurance_Corporation).According to FDIC.gov (as of March 2013), "FDIC deposit insurance is backed by the full faith and credit of the United States government. This means that the resources of the United States government stand behind FDIC-insured depositors." The statutory basis for this claim is less than clear. Congress, in 1987, passed a non-binding "Sense of Congress" to that effect, but there appear to be no laws strictly binding the government to make good on any insurance liabilities unmet by the FDIC.

contributions are no longer needed (see Article 69 of the SRM Regulation). But this implies that the incentive effect of linking contributions to risk factors at the individual bank level no longer operates once the target level has been reached at the level of the overall fund.

The problem can be solved in two ways (see Box 1). One way would be to keep assessing contributions even after the fund has reached its target level, but provide banks with a refund based on their past contributions. The ongoing contributions would then be based on *current* risk levels (in terms of riskiness and magnitude of insured deposits), thus providing the right incentives.

Box 1. Contributions to a bank resolution fund: Conceptual underpinnings

The usual approach is to set the annual flow, i.e. the contribution of each bank for each year, as simply a function of its liabilities base (of that year) and certain risk factors (measured for that year or some recent past average):

$$contribution_{i,t} = \alpha_{i,t}(riskfactors)L_{i,t}$$

where the alpha denotes the contribution rate of bank i, which will be a function of its riskiness. The liabilities base on which contribution rates, alpha, are defined is not material for the problem at hand. The alpha can be calibrated in such a way that the target level of the fund is reached in a number of years (ten in Europe).

The main limitation of this approach is that contributions stop when the target level has been reached, i.e. when the sum of all past contributions (neglecting interest the fund earns on its investments) is larger than the target level.

$$\sum_{t,i} c_{i,t} \geq overall\ target\ level = x\left[\sum_i L_i\right]/100$$

In the case of Europe, the target level would be equal to a percentage x of the liabilities base, which has to be calculated as a function of the ratio between covered deposits and the liability base for contributions (x = covered deposits/liabilities). After 10 years, contributions would thus stop and the risk factors would cease to have an incentive effect.

A simple way to ensure that the incentive effect of risk-based contributions is preserved beyond the transition period is to stipulate that the annual contributions have to be paid each year, irrespective of the size of the fund. But there would be an additional rule: each bank also receives a transfer back which is proportional to its share in the total pot accumulated so far.

Under this computationally simple way to preserve the incentive effects of risk-based contributions, the annual net transfer a bank has to make to the resolution fund would be calculated thus:

$$net\ payment = nc_{i,T} = c_{i,T} - \frac{\sum_{t=0}^{T} c_{i,t}}{Target\ level}$$

where $\sum_{t=0}^{T} c_{i,t}$ denotes the sum of all past payments made by bank i.

Under this system the incentive effects of the risk-based factors would persist even after the target level has been reached.

The net amount a bank would have to transfer to the system, i.e. the difference between its annual contribution and its pro rata reimbursement, could thus become negative (and indeed on average half of the banks would face net negative 'contributions').

Alternative approach:

At time t the overall target stock of capital bank i should have contributed to the resolution fund is defined as:

$$C_{i,t}^* = \alpha_{i,t}(riskfactors)L_{i,t}$$

where the alpha denotes again the contribution rate of bank i, which should be a function of its risk factors (capital base, etc.).

The annual contribution bank i would have to transfer to the resolution fund could be one-tenth of the difference between the target capital level and the sum of the actual transfer bank i has made in the past (neglecting interest the fund earned, which would have to be offset against its running costs).

Formally, the annual contribution, denoted by a lower case c, in year T, would be given by:

$$c_{i,T} = \frac{\left[C_{i,T}^* - \sum_{t=0}^{T} c_{i,t}\right]}{10}$$

Under this system the incentive effects of the risk-based factors would remain intact even after the resolution fund has reached its target level of 1% of covered deposits. Banks whose risk has fallen relative to the past would receive a reimbursement and banks whose riskiness has increased would continue to have to pay. The same applies to increases/falls in the liabilities which form the base for the contribution: banks whose liabilities increase (more than the system average) continue to pay whereas those whose liability base falls receive reimbursements.

Another approach would be to define a target *level* for the stake each bank has in the resolution fund. This stake is given by the sum of its past contributions to the fund. As shown in Box 1, this would be subtly different from the usual approach of defining an annual contribution based on present risk levels.

The box also shows that if one wants to preserve the incentive effects of risk-based contributions beyond the transition period, one needs to keep the annual contributions, irrespective of the size of the fund. But, to keep the fund limited, there would be an additional rule that, once the target level has been reached, each bank *also* receives a transfer back in proportion to its share in the total pot accumulated so far. Under this approach the incentive effects of the risk-based factors would persist even after the target level has been reached.

The net amount a bank would have to transfer to the system, i.e. the difference between its annual contribution and its pro rata reimbursement, could thus become negative for those banks whose risk profile improves. (In a no-growth situation. on average. half of the banks would face net negative 'contributions'.)

One needs thus to make a clear distinction between the annual flows of payments to the fund (contributions) and the stock of cumulated contributions to the fund which denote for each bank the stake or capital that the bank has contributed to the fund in the past. Unfortunately, this principle has not been recognised in the agreement of 21 October 2014, on the "ex-ante contributions to the Single Resolution Fund" (http://ec.europa.eu/internal_market/finances/banking-union/single-resolution-mechanism/index_en.htm). The contributions to the SRM will thus not contribute to pricing risk-taking by individual banks once the target level of the funds has been reached.

6.3 Separating resolution and deposit insurance: Principles of a two-tier European deposit (re)insurance system

As mentioned above, it is widely agreed that a full banking union comprises three elements, namely common supervision, common funding for restructuring and common deposit insurance. Many academic observers (see, for example, the contributions to Beck, 2012) stress the need to introduce all three elements together. However, deposit insurance has de facto been dropped from the official agenda.[23]

This does not imply that nothing has been done regarding deposit insurance at the EU level. The European Commission tabled a proposal for a directive on DGS in 2010.[24] The directive has in the meantime been adopted (http://ec.europa.eu/ internal_market/bank/guarantee/index_en.htm).

However, the scope of this 'DGS' directive is quite limited as it aims only at harmonising coverage, the arrangements for pay-out, e.g. the time limit for paying out depositors, and the financing of national DGSs. The Commission has so far only proposed "mutual borrowing between DGSs, i.e. a borrowing facility in certain circumstances". Somewhat surprisingly, an accompanying Joint Research Centre report (JRC, 2011) on

---

[23] The blueprint of the European Commission for a 'genuine EMU' contains only a passing reference to the need for "solid deposit guarantee schemes in all Member States". Some have argued that it is not needed and others that it is just politically too contentious, e.g. Pisani-Ferry & Wolf (2012).

[24] http://ec.europa.eu/internal_market/bank/docs/guarantee/ 20100712_proposal_en.pdf.

deposit insurance at the EU level does not consider the reinsurance model at all. [25]

The case for maintaining deposit insurance at the national level used to be that the national level remains best qualified to evaluate idiosyncratic risks of the banks under its watch. National DGSs should also have the right incentive to monitor individual banks as they would have to pay for any losses. In reality, however, most national DGSs (and national supervisors in general) operate within so many political constraints that they have little influence, except on very small banks. At any rate, with supervision now concentrated in the SSM (effectively the ECB) the case of retaining deposit insurance has been fundamentally weakened.

The fact that the ECB will be the *direct* supervisor of only the largest 120 banks might strengthen the case of leaving all the other smaller banks under national deposit insurance, but the SRM will cover all banks.

Moreover, a little noticed part of the SRM agreement stipulates that the SRM can require (national) DGSs to make a contribution to the resolution of banks up to the amount of the losses the DGS would have made if the SRM had not intervened, i.e. the bank would have gone into insolvency. This makes sense from a theoretical point of view: if the SRM puts its funds into a bank and thus helps a DGS to avoid a loss, this advantage for the DGS should be compensated. However, while this approach seems theoretically logical it is likely to be totally impractical because the amount the DGS(s) would have to contribute to the resolution of a bank under the SRM would have to be determined in a few hours during a frantic a weekend.

---

[25] Under the heading "Pan-EU DGS", this report "explored the option to establish a pan-EU DGS, either:

a. in the form of a single entity replacing the existing schemes, or

b. in the form of a complementary fund to existing DGS ('28th regime'), or

c. structured as a network of schemes providing each other with mutual assistance ('European system of DGS')."

Moreover, the determination of how much a DGS would have lost in case the SRM had not intervened (and the bank thus would have gone into insolvency) can never be determined objectively.

This is not just a general consideration, but a real life problem. When the Icelandic banks went insolvent, institutions had collected deposits in several countries. Although these banks had operated through branches, the national authorities felt compelled to compensate savers in their country as if the branches had been covered by the national DGS (because the Icelandic deposit insurance system also became effectively insolvent). At the time (2008), it appeared that his would impose a great cost on national taxpayers in Germany, the UK and the Netherlands. However, the end result was quite different from the initial fears. The German DGS was able to recover most of the cost it incurred compensating German savers because it was able to seize some assets in Germany and then wait patiently until these assets recovered in value. The UK and Dutch governments brought a court case against the Icelandic government, as they were not able to recover any assets in their countries. However, over time the estate of the Icelandic banks was able to recover much more than initially assumed, given that depositors had a preference over many other creditors. More than one half of the losses have thus already been covered. The FDIC has had a similar experience in recent years. In some cases it had to revise its losses considerably downwards over time.

In real life insolvency cases the estimates of the recovery value of assets can thus vary greatly over time. However, if the SRM intervenes the cost of insolvency cannot be observed and can only be estimated as a counterfactual. There will thus be an unavoidable conflict of interest between the SRM and (national) DGS.

These difficulties would of course multiply for internationally active banks (with different subsidiaries in different countries, which remains the dominant model). The SRM would thus have to determine over a weekend how much each national DGS would have to contribute in an insolvency of the group. This seems next to impossible given that one would have to determine what assets would be a disposable for different national authorities – a process that would likely take years and many lengthy court cases.

The cases of the Icelandic banks and of the *cajas* in Spain shows that the real problem in deposit insurance is not the problems posed by individual banks, but by system risk. Experience confirms again and again that national authorities are not well placed to evaluate systemic risk, i.e. risks to their entire banking system. As discussed extensively above, the main source of such shocks which often threaten the entire national banking system are local real estate booms and busts.

The national real estate bubbles were not recognised as such in Spain or Ireland, although foreign observers and EU institutions had repeatedly warned about unsustainable developments. Moreover, national authorities are also not well placed in practice to deal with banks that are well connected at the national political level, either because of size ('national champions') or because of the nature of their business (banks financing local real estate development). This fosters the accumulation of large risks and delays in loss recognition once the bubble bursts. A local real estate bubble which had been financed by local institutions with local deposits might also constitute a case in which the SRM might thus be the most likely case under which a large number of local banks would incur large losses with high pay-outs required from the national DGS.

There is thus a need to reinsure national deposit insurance systems against large, systemic events.[26]

The need for reinsurance thus arises even without considering the specific problems posed by large cross-border bank groups. In reality, most large cross-border banks operate via subsidiaries. These subsidiaries contribute to the DGS of their host countries the same way as purely national banks do, and the national DGS would have to pay out should one of these large

---

[26] Pisani-Ferry et al. (2012) arrive at the same conclusion.

cross-border banks fail. This provides some automatic burden-sharing.

However, the burden-sharing is limited to the case of cross-border banks operating with subsidiaries. Losses at large cross-border banking groups (mostly classified as SIFIs, or significantly important financial institutions) pose other problems, as the distribution of assets across subsidiaries will determine where the losses arise. The experience with Fortis has clearly shown this phenomenon. SIFIs are usually saved by government intervention because of the threat they pose to systemic stability.

Deposit insurers are thus not directly involved and anyway do not constitute the largest creditors because these large institutions are mostly universal banks for which deposit-taking is only one part of the overall business model with customer deposits amounting usually to less than one-half of the balance sheet. Figure 8 below shows the share of customer deposits by bank size (measured as total assets) of the more than 100 euro area banks subjected to at least one of the Committee of European Banking Supervisors (CEBS) and European Bank Authority (EBA) exercises between 2010 and 2014 or the ECB Comprehensive Assessment in 2014, which covered for all the member countries the largest banks accounting for at least one-half of assets at the national level.[27]

---

[27] The 2010 stress test exercise was conducted on a sample of 91 European banks. In total, national supervisory authorities from 20 EU member states participated in the exercise. In each of the 27 member states, the sample was built by including banks, in descending order of size, so as to cover at least 50% of the respective national banking sector, as expressed in terms of total assets. As the stress test was conducted at the highest level of consolidation for the bank in question, the exercise also covers subsidiaries and branches of these EU banks operating in other member states and in countries outside Europe. As a result, for the remaining seven member states where more than 50% of the local market was already covered through the subsidiaries of EU banks participating in the exercise, no further bank was added to the sample. The 91 banks represent 65% of the total assets of the EU banking sector as a whole. For about 10 of these banks no data on customer deposits was available.

Figure 8. The relative importance of deposits as a function of bank size

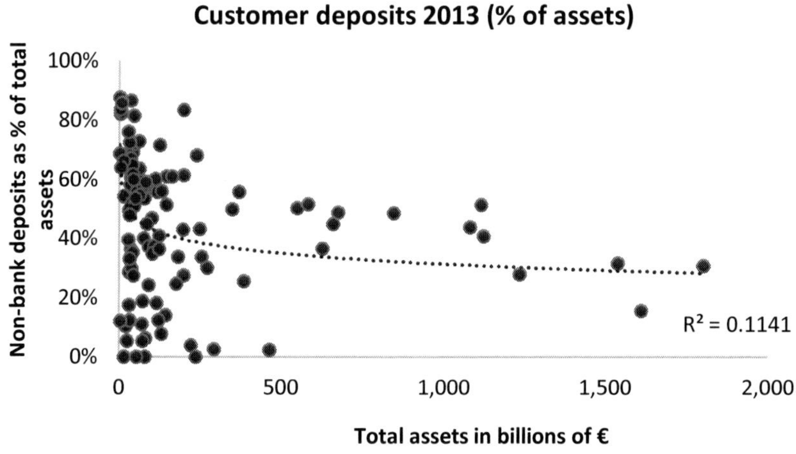

Customer deposits 2013 (% of assets)

Source: CEPS database (see Ayadi & De Groen, 2014).

Existing mutual guarantee schemes provide another rationale for reinsurance. These schemes, notably among the German savings banks, exist usually among groups of small savings institutions, all of which have a very similar business model. Groups of banks with a mutual guarantee system constitute essentially one large bank from the point of view of a deposit insurance system. There is no reason to dissolve systems that have worked well so far. But these groups clearly are not immune to systemic risk. A first reinsurance layer for groups of savings or cooperative banks which have a mutual guarantee agreement could be provided at the national level. But this is not sufficient since these groups account for a large share of deposits in some countries and could thus overtax the loss absorption capacity of the national authorities.

There has been some debate about the need for a European approach to deposit insurance (for a survey see Belke, 2014). For example, Pisani-Ferry & Wolff (2012) argued that a common deposit insurance fund is not needed. The reason given was that deposit funds insure against the failure of a single, small financial institution, but not against the failure of the euro area financial system. This is undoubtedly true. But their argument actually strengthens the case made here for the need for some backup for national DGSs that experience a shock that is systemic at the national level, but not at the euro area level. The experience with Spain and Ireland has shown that this type of shock can certainly arise. Depositor confidence everywhere should be strengthened if it is known that there exists a credible backup for national deposit insurance funds.[28]

Box 2. The FDIC as an example for Europe?

The Federal Deposit Insurance Corporation (FDIC) in the US is an independent institution with a considerable staff which can monitor and assess the risk posed by the thousands individual banks operating in the US.

A key aspect of the FDIC is that it is completely unconcerned by the local political difficulties that might arise when it swoops in and resolves an ailing bank over a weekend. During this crisis the FDIC has been able to resolve hundreds of (admittedly mostly small) banks, whereas in Europe very few banks have been resolved or allowed to fail. However, some of the banks dealt with by the FDIC had balance sheets which were larger than those of the banks in Cyprus and even most *cajas* in Spain. What qualifies as small for the FDIC (and probably for the SRM as well) could thus be relevant in the context of smaller member states.

The FDIC follows a strict 'waterfall' of claims with junior debt first to be wiped out and even senior bondholders often suffering large haircuts. The FDIC model would thus be preferable for the EU as well, but unfortunately it does not seem to have any chance of being adopted at present.

---

[28] If a common deposit insurance of this form remains absent due to worries about moral hazard, the euro area will most likely remain less integrated financially. This is because the scope for private financial flows to accommodate asymmetric shocks would be restricted. Credit institutions would stay retrenched within national boundaries, limiting the supply of credit in weaker economies, inhibiting their capacity to restore growth and employment. See Begg (2014) and Howarth & Quaglia (2013).

It is interesting to note that one of the key arguments for the creation of the FDIC was the fact that deposit guarantee had been a responsibility of the states. But during the crisis of the early 1930s, most of the deposit schemes at the state level had become insolvent (Golembe, 1960) as contagion led to a cascade of local banking panics which overwhelmed the capacity of the local DGSs of the time.

One of the key reasons why state deposit insurance systems failed was that the small undiversified banks exposed to local real estate bubbles and agricultural difficulties were prone to systemic crisis (Thies & Gerlowski, 1989). This problem remains even today. The Spanish and Irish deposit insurance funds would be overwhelmed by the multiple failures within a small undiversified group of banks resulting from a local boom and bust. Federal reinsurance would diversify this risk of local shocks.

The need to provide insurance against systemic shocks remains today as important as ever. This need motivates the following concrete proposal.

6.4 Basic principles of reinsurance

Gros (2013) proposes to apply the principles of subsidiarity and reinsurance to deposit insurance. The basic idea is simple: Existing national DGSs would continue to operate much as before (with only minimal standards set by an EU directive), but they would be required to take out reinsurance against risks that would be too large to be covered by them. A 'European Reinsurance Fund' (EReIF) would provide this reinsurance financed by premia paid by the national DGSs, just as any reinsurance company does in the private sector. The EReIF would pay out only in case of large losses. This 'deductible' would provide the national authorities with the proper incentives, but the reinsurance cover would stabilise depositor confidence even in the case of large shocks.[29]

---

[29] It will of course take time to build up the funding for such a reinsurance fund. This approach is thus not meant to deal with legacy problems from the current crisis.

A first point is that what is needed is reinsurance, not a mutual guarantee among all national DGSs. This implies that the reinsurance scheme proposed here will not put the deposits of savers in 'virtuous' countries at risk – their potential losses would be limited to their share in the common fund.

Three other principles also need to be stressed: the compulsory nature, the need for independent management and premia based on systemic, or macroeconomic risk, and the transition.

6.4.1 Compulsory reinsurance with a deductible

The *compulsory* element is indispensable. Otherwise, a serious adverse selection bias would arise. Differences in risk profiles are no reason to allow any national DGS to opt out.

(National) *Deductible*: As for any insurance, there should be a first loss tranche, or deductible, which is borne at the national level. This means that the losses that might arise if a small- to medium-sized bank fails would have to be covered by the national DGS alone. This 'deductible' should be of such a size that the national DGS could pay out without endangering its own viability. It should be proportional to the size of the national fund accumulated, which in turn should be large enough to deal with the failure of any single domestic bank (but not necessarily the EU-wide deposits of the large cross-border banking groups). The Commission has proposed to set as a target for each national DGS a fund equivalent to 1.5% of (insured) deposits. The national DGSs should then dedicate a part of the risk premia they collect from their banks to reinsure themselves with the EReIF. As a rough guess, about one-third to one-half of the premia collected at the national level might be needed for the reinsurance against systemic or large national shocks.

The contract between the EReIF and the national DGS would thus specify that the EReIF would pay out if, over a period to be specified (say two or three years), the total claims on the national DGS exceed by, e.g. two times, the fund accumulated nationally. Another way to specify the reinsurance event would be to fix the deductible (or national first loss piece) in terms of a percentage of GDP.

Reinsurance is thus completely different from lending among national DGSs, as proposed by the European Commission. A national DGS will need financial support only if the country experiences a systemic crisis. But these are exactly the conditions under which the other DGS systems will not want to lend and it will be difficult to force the stronger DGSs to lend to others in crisis. Moreover, this mutual lending will constitute a vehicle for contagion, which should be avoided.[30]

There will be limits to the amount the EReIF pays out. The limit is likely to be large enough to cover systemic events in small- to medium-sized member states. The empirical literature indicates that the average cost of a banking crisis is around 5% of GDP. Even for a country like Spain, this would translate into €50 billion, and should thus be manageable by a fund of this order of magnitude.

A systemic shock to a large country could not be handled by the EReIF alone. In such a case, recourse to the ESM will be unavoidable because any systemic crisis of a large member country will lead to systemic consequences for the entire euro area economy. It will then be up to the fiscal authorities represented in the ESM to decide whether European taxpayers' money should be used to intervene.

How much protection could be provided by the reinsurance model proposed here? If one assumes that one-half of the premia are needed to cover systematic risk, the protection provided by the EReIF would be inverse to the size of the country. For example, for a small country which accounts only for 5% of all deposits, the common fund would be 20 times as large as the national fund. Even for a country accounting for 10% of all deposits, e.g. Spain, the EReIF would still be 10 times larger than the national fund and thus be much more able to deal with a loss that might be too large to be dealt with at the national level.

---

[30] A 2011 study of the Joint Research Centre (JRC) of the EU did not consider the reinsurance approach. See Joint Research Centre (2011).

6.4.2   Premiums and management

Risk premia should of course reflect differences in risk. Systemic events materialise rarely. It will thus be very difficult to calculate the appropriate premia. There will be long periods during which no systemic event occurs, and of course it is hoped that many countries will never experience a systemic crisis in a given lifetime. But one could use the expertise of the large European reinsurance industry to assess the proper premium for this type of rare event. A real institution will be needed; a mere 'post box' system without expertise at the centre will not work because it would not be able to properly assess the risk of the national DGS. It is of course essential that the institution that sets the premia for the reinsurance is completely independent of political influence in its risk assessment. This seems to exclude the ESM in its present form because its staff has little autonomy under a board that is dominated by the national finance ministers whose main mandate is to look after the interests of their national taxpayers, and not the stability of the whole system.

The EReIF would not need to have expert knowledge in bank management, but would need to look out for systemic, macroeconomic risk. In principle, this expertise is already available in the ESRB. It would thus be important to find an institutional solution under which this expertise can be used by the EReIF. For example, the EReIF could be empowered to increase the premia it charges the national DGSs concerned if the national authorities had ignored a warning and a recommendation from the ESRB to undertake certain actions to forestall a potential danger to price stability.[31]

The EReIF should also be able to judge the overall quality of the national DGSs, which requires expertise in systems management, rather than analysts of bank balance sheets. The EReIF should thus have the right to inspect the practical working

---

[31] A warning under the excessive imbalances procedure (EIP), which is managed by the Commission and decided by the ECOFIN Council, could of course be taken as another signal to the EReIF that the DGS of the country in question faces a greater risk of a systemic event.

of national DGSs, checking for example whether premia are properly adjusted for risk (as required already by the EU Directive on DGS). Here it could benefit from the expertise of the Directorate General for Competition Policy (DG Comp) of the European Commission. In the private sector such supervision of the reinsured is usually not feasible. This is why a fundamental principle of private reinsurance contracts is "The Duty of Utmost Good Faith" (Devery & Farrell, 2008).[32] Under this principle, the EReIF should be present at the table once a national DGS is nearing the borderline where a pay-out from the EReIF would be triggered. The EReIF would then need to give its consent to measures that would reduce loss-absorption capacity. Here again, a collaboration with DG Comp would make sense.

6.4.3 Transition

For a two-tier system like the one proposed here, the transition should be relatively straightforward to manage. Presumably there will be no need for immediate pay-outs (assuming no systemic crisis arises again). This implies that the reinsurance function can be built up gradually as do the funds in the EReIF.

The legacy problems from the current crisis should have been dealt with in the meantime by the Asset Quality Review which the ECB conducted in 2014 prior to becoming the direct supervisor of the 120 largest euro area banks.

A new, two-tier deposit insurance system could thus start anytime, with the EReIF gradually building up its capital. The next systemic crisis will be different from the euro crisis and, it is hoped, far enough in the future to allow enough time to build a new institution and accumulate enough funding to counter it.

---

[32] "One of the most fundamental principles in reinsurance – indeed, what sets the reinsurance field apart from most other industries – is the concept of utmost good faith (also known as 'uberrimae fides'). The duty originated in the context of marine insurance law, when underwriters had no practical means of inspecting reinsured ships or cargo in distant ports."

7. GENERAL CONSIDERATIONS: FISCAL UNION AND FINANCIAL SHOCK ABSORBER

A key finding of this study is that a common backup system for banks combined with the overall integration of national financial systems greatly increase the ability of financial markets to reduce the negative spillovers among members of a monetary union resulting from national or regional financial crisis. This finding is confirmed in more macroeconomic terms by the empirical literature which measures the channels of stabilisation of regional income in existing monetary unions, like the US and Germany. For example, Asdrubali, Sorensen & Yosha (1996) find that in the US, around 40% of shocks to per capita GSP is smoothed by capital markets and around 25% by credit markets. This implies that about two-thirds of shocks to state income are absorbed by financial markets. Similarly, Athanasoulis & van Wincoop (2001) find that around 70% of the shocks in the US are smoothed through private and public risk-sharing mechanisms: financial markets play the biggest role, allowing around 60% of the total smoothing of income after a shock, while the federal fiscal policy covers the other 10%. More recently, Hepp & von Hagen (2013) find that for Germany, in the pre-unification period, most of the smoothing was provided by the federal tax-transfer and grant system (55%), while for the post-unification period, factor income flows have become the most important channel (contributing about 51% of total income smoothing).

The introduction of the euro and the common payments infrastructure has reduced barriers to financial integration, and credit flows via the wholesale interbank market have boosted financial integration as measured by the size of cross-border flows and stocks. This was expected to facilitate risk-sharing among investors.

However, the euro crisis has shown that sometimes larger cross-border financial flows and stock can actually be at the origin of a crisis (Mink & de Haan, 2014). The main reason for this is that banks have been the primary financial intermediaries in the European Union and in the euro area. Most euro area member countries' financial systems are heavily 'bank-centred' and stock and bond markets provide a relatively modest share of the financing to the private sector in most countries. Total bank assets account for 283% of GDP in the EU, compared to about 65% of GDP in the US (Fuceri & Zdzienicka, 2013).

There is no robust evidence in the literature that such a financial system, dominated by banks (rather than markets) and debt (instead of equity), has increased the capacity of the economy for risk-sharing.

Kalemli-Ozcan et al. (2010) and Demyank et al. (2007) find evidence that increased cross-banking integration has fostered ex post the optimality of the currency union by improving cross-country risk-sharing. By contrast, Furceri (2013) finds that "the decrease in private credit smoothing after the creation of the EMU reflects the fact that credit flows have become less counter-cyclical".

By contrast, as is the main focus of this paper, the US shows how a high degree of banking integration can absorb shocks. The main reason for this is that banking integration in the US has not taken the form of cross-border credit, but de facto cross-border equity, as a few large banks are operating nationwide.

8. CONCLUDING REMARKS

The existing banking union in the US has been very successful in managing local real estate booms and busts. A careful comparison of the cases of Nevada and Florida (compared to Ireland and Spain, respectively) showed that these financial shock absorbers have a higher shock-absorbing capacity than could ever be provided by any common budget ('fiscal capacity') for the euro area. The macroeconomic literature confirms this in the sense that it shows that in the US, the shock absorption provided by financial markets is much larger than that provided by the fiscal system (see, for instance, Begg, 2014).

There are several channels through which regional financial shocks are absorbed at the federal level in the US. The FDIC is the most visible one, but the system of securitisation of mortgages, especially the 'GSEs', contributes as well. Moreover, the large banks, which operate nationwide, dominate the banking sector. They are able to absorb local losses in their overall results. By contrast, in Europe large banks operating in different member countries are still perceived as foreign banks outside their home country. Integration via international groups has so far been limited in the euro area (but has been, as shown above as a quasi-banking union, very important for the new member states).

The prevalent form of financial market integration across borders within the euro area is debt, which does not act as a shock absorber in the case of systemic shocks. By contrast there has been much more cross-border equity outside the euro area through large-scale foreign ownership of banks in Central and Eastern Europe.

If the really important and costly shocks are national financial boom-bust cycles, followed by a financial crisis, the question arises: What arrangement provides the best protection against these shocks?

The US experience seems to provide a clear answer: the shock-absorbing power of explicit federal transfers to specific federal states is rather small, but the US banking union provides important support in the case of large shocks to the local financial system.

This has one simple implication: to insure its stability, the euro area needs a strong banking union, but not a fiscal union.[33] The usual argument that the former needs to be followed by the latter should thus be turned on its head: an area with a well-functioning banking union has much less need for fiscal shock absorbers and does not need a fiscal union (see also Belke, 2013, 2013a). From the latter, it follows that there is also no need for a political union.

It is of course possible, indeed likely, that the limited funding available for the euro area bank resolution fund (the SRF) might prove insufficient in the event that a large member country experiences a deep crisis. In this case the SRF might need a fiscal backstop, much as the FDIC needed a line of credit from the US Treasury when its losses exceeded, temporarily, its financial base. Such a backstop could be provided by the ESM, but it does not seem appropriate to create a fiscal union just to be double sure that there is enough common funding for a once in a generation crisis.

This study has concentrated on shocks resulting from regional boom-bust cycles. There are of course other sources of shocks. The case of Greece has illustrated what can go wrong if a government overspends and accumulates excessive debt. Gros (2015) argues that even in this case a banking union can help to moderate the shock to the financial system. He shows that the default of Puerto Rico (practically a fully-fledged state of the US)

---

[33] For an early discussion of fiscal and political union, see Gros & Thygesen (1995). The view that a fiscal and political union is needed is expressed at the political level by the report of the four EU Presidents on Genuine Economic and Monetary Union (Van Rompuy et al., 2012).

occurred without major financial market disruption in Puerto Rico itself because of the fact that the banking system there was safeguarded by the US FDIC.

In a banking union, excessive spending by individual member states should ideally lead to difficulties for the state concerned, but it should no longer destabilise the entire system. This implies that political responsibility for fiscal policy can remain at the national level. Technically speaking, one can thus argue that a banking union significantly reduces the negative external effects of excessive deficits and debts. The EU banking union thus represents a key element in making the original Maastricht view, with its 'no bail out clause', viable in reality.

Two elements of the US banking union that do not exist, at least not yet, in the euro area are widespread securitisation and the existence of large banks that operate throughout the entire area. These two characteristics of the US financial system present important additional shock absorbers and lessen the need for fiscal backstops for the federal institutions.

But these two characteristics also have their own drawbacks. Large banks are often more prone to generate systemic risk, and it has been shown (ASC, 2014) that most of the growth in the banking sector over the last decade has come from the largest banks. The drawbacks of widespread securitisation also became apparent during the 'sub-prime' crisis, when it was shown that the originating banks were subject to serious conflicts of interest as they earned fees from originating mortgages irrespective of the quality of the borrower and his/her ability to service the loans. A system that deals more easily with regional crises might thus have other drawbacks.

The challenge for Europe will be to build a system that breaks the 'diabolical' feedback loop between weak banks and their sovereign but also one that is not dominated by a handful of very big banks which are not only too big to fail, but also too big to be saved.

REFERENCES

Acharya, V.V. and T. Yorulmazer (2007), "Too Many to Fail: An Analysis of Time-Inconsistency in Bank Closure Policies", Working Paper no. 319, Bank of England, February.

Advisory Scientific Committee (ASC) (2014), "Is Europe Overbanked?", Reports of the Advisory Scientific Committee of the ESRB, No. 4, European Systemic Risk Board, Frankfurt, June (www.esrb.europa.eu/pub/pdf/asc/Reports_ASC_4_1406.pdf).

Aizenman, J. (2012), "US Banking over Two Centuries: Lessons for the Eurozone Crisis", in T. Beck (ed.), *Banking Union for Europe: Risks and Challenges*, London: Centre for Economic Policy Research (www.voxeu.org/content/banking-union-europe-risks-and-challenges).

Allard, C., P.K. Brooks, J.C. Bluedorn, F. Bornhorst, K. Christopherson, F. Ohnsorge and T. Poghosyan (2013), "Towards a Fiscal Union for the Euro Area", IMF Staff Discussion Note 13/09, International Monetary Fund, Washington, D.C., November.

Asdrubali, P., B.E. Sorensen and O. Yosha (1996), "Channels of Interstate Risk Sharing: United States 1963-1990", *Quarterly Journal of Economics*, Vol. 111(4), November, pp. 1081-1110.

Athanasoulis, S. and E. van Wincoop (2001), "Risk Sharing within the United States: What Do Financial Markets and Fiscal Federalism Accomplish?", *Review of Economics and Statistics*, Vol. 83(4), November, pp. 688-698.

Ayadi, R. and W.P. de Groen (2014), "Banking Business Models Monitor 2014: Europe", Joint Centre for European Policy Studies (CEPS) and International Observatory on Financial Service Cooperatives (IOFSC) publication, Montreal.

Beck, T., D. Gros and D. Schoenmaker (2013), "On the Design of a Single Resolution Mechanism", European Parliament, Monetary Dialogue Notes (www.europarl.europa.eu/ document/activities/cont/201304/20130422ATT64861/2 0130422ATT64861EN.pdf).

Beck, T. (ed.) (2012), *Banking Union for Europe: Risks and Challenges*, London: Centre for Economic Policy Research (http://www.voxeu.org/content/banking-union-europe-risks-and-challenges).

Begg, I. (2014), "Genuine Economic and Monetary Union", in S.N. Durlauf and L.E. Blume (eds), *The New Palgrave Dictionary of Economics Online*, Basingstoke: Palgrave Macmillan (www.dictionaryofeconomics.com/ article?id=pde2014_E000339).

Belke, A. (2013), "Towards a Genuine Economic and Monetary Union – Comments on a Roadmap", *Politics and Governance*, Vol. 1(1), pp. 48-65.

_____ (2013a), "Debt Mutualisation in the Ongoing Eurozone Crisis – A Tale of the 'North' and the 'South'", S.N. Durlauf and L.E. Blume (eds), *The New Palgrave Dictionary of Economics Online*, Basingstoke: Palgrave Macmillan (www.dictionaryofeconomics.com/article?id=pde2013_D 000273).

_____ (2014), "Oral Evidence", in House of Lords EU Economic and Financial Affairs Sub-committee, *Genuine Economic and Monetary Union Evidence*, 8th Report of Session 2013-14, London: The Stationery Office.

Bignon, V., R. Breton and M.R. Breu (2013), "Currency Union with and without Banking Union", Banque de France Working Paper 450, Banque de France, Paris, October.

Breuss, F., W. Roeger and J. in'tVeld (2014), "The Stabilising Properties of a European Banking Union in Case of Financial Shocks in the Euro Area", DG ECFIN Economic Papers.

Buch, C.M., T. Körner and B. Weigert (2013), "Towards Deeper Financial Integration in Europe: What the Banking Union Can Contribute", Working Paper 02/2013, German Council of Economic Advisors, Wiesbaden, August.

Chari, V.V., and P. Kehoe (2009) "Bailouts, Time Inconsistency and Optimal Regulation," Federal Reserve Bank of Minneapolis Research Department Staff Report, November.

Demyank, Y., C. Ostergaard and B. Sorensen (2007), "Risk Sharing and Portfolio Allocation in EMU", European Commission Working Paper, Brussels.

Devery, J.R. and E.M. Farrell (2008), "Key Principles and Concepts", in *Mealey's Fundamentals of Reinsurance Litigation & Arbitration*, 11 February, Washington, D.C.

European Commission (2012), A Blueprint for a Deep and Genuine Economic and Monetary Union Launching a European Debate, Communication from the Commission, Brussels, 28.11.2012 COM(2012) 777 final.

FDIC (1997), "An Examination of the Banking Crises of the 1980s and Early 1990s", Federal Deposit Insurance Corporation, Washington, D.C. (www.fdic.gov/bank/historical/history/137_165.pdf).

Furceri, D. and A. Zdzienicka (2013), "The Euro Area Crisis: Need for a Supranational Fiscal Risk Sharing Mechanism?", IMF Working Paper WP/13/198, International Monetary Fund, Washington, D.C., September.

Gimber, A.R. (2012), "Bank Resolution, Bailouts and the Time Consistency Problem", mimeo, European University Institute, Florence.

Golembe, C. (1960), "The Deposit Insurance Legislation of 1933", *Political Science Quarterly*, 76, pp. 181-195.

Grochulsky, B. (2011), "Financial Firm Resolution Policy as a Time-Consistency Problem", *FRBR Economic Quarterly*, Vol. 97(2), pp. 133-152.

Gros, D. (2012a), "Principles of a Two-Tier European Deposit (Re-) Insurance System", *Kredit und Kapital*, Vol. 45, No. 4, pp. 489-499.

_____ (2012b), "Banking Union: Ireland vs. Nevada, an illustration of the importance of an integrated banking system", CEPS Commentary, Centre for European Policy Studies, Brussels, October (www.ceps.eu/book/banking-union-ireland-vs-nevada-illustration-importance-integrated-banking-system).

_____ (2013), "The SRM and the Dream to Resolve Banks without Public Money", CEPS Commentary, Centre for European Policy Studies, Brussels, 19 December.

_____ (2015) "Puerto Rico and Greece: A tale of two defaults in a monetary union", CEPS High Level Brief, 30 June, CEPS, Brussels (www.ceps.eu/publications/puerto-rico-and-greece-tale-two-defaults-monetary-union).

Gros, D. and D. Schoenmaker (2012), "European Deposit Insurance: Financing the Transition", CEPS Commentary, 6 September (www.ceps.eu/book/european-deposit-insurance-financing-transition).

_____ (2013), "Cleaning up the Mess: Bank Resolution in a Systemic Crisis", CEPS Commentary, CEPS, Brussels, 7 June.

Gros, D. and N. Thygesen (1995), *European Monetary Integration*, London: Longman.

Hepp, R. and J. von Hagen (2013), "Interstate Risk-sharing in Germany: 1970-2006", *Oxford Economic Papers*, 65(1), January, pp. 1-24.

Howarth, D. and L. Quaglia (2013), "Banking Union as Holy Grail: Rebuilding the Single Market in Financial Services, Stabilizing Europe's Banks and 'Completing' Economic and Monetary Union", *Journal of Common Market Studies*, Vol. 51, pp. 103-123.

IMF (2013a), "A Banking Union for the Euro Area", IMF Staff Discussion Note 13/01, International Monetary Fund, Washington, D.C., February.

_____ (2013b), "Toward a Fiscal Union for the Euro Area", IMF Staff Discussion Note 13/09, International Monetary Fund, Washington, D.C., September.

Ingves, S. (2010), "The Crisis in the Baltic – the Riksbank's Measures, Assessments and Lessons Learned", Speech by Mr Stefan Ingves, Governor of the Sveriges Riksbank, to the Riksdag Committee on Finance, Stockholm, 2 February (www.bis.org/review/r100203b.pdf).

Joint Research Centre (JRC) (2011), "JRC Report under Article 12 of Directive 94/19/EC as amended by Directive 2009/14/EC", Joint Research Centre, European Commission, Unit G09, Ispra (Italy) (http://ec.europa.eu/internal_market/bank/docs/guarantee/jrc-rep_en.pdf).

Kalemli-Ozcan, S., E. Papaioannou and J.L. Peydró (2010), "What Lies beneath the Euro's Effect on Financial Integration? Currency Risk, Legal Harmonization, or Trade?", *Journal of International Economics*, 81(1), pp. 75-88.

McArdle, P. (2012), "The Euro Crisis: Refinancing the Irish bailout – the options post the June 2012 Summit", IIEA Working Paper, Institute of International and European Affairs, Dublin.

Mink, M. and J. de Haan (2014), "Spillovers from Systemic Bank Defaults", CESifo Working Paper 4792, CESifo, Munich, May.

Pisani-Ferry, J. and G.B. Wolff (2012), "The Fiscal Implications of a Banking Union", Bruegel Policy Brief No. 2012/02, Bruegel, Brussels.

Pisani-Ferry, J., A. Sapir, N. Véron and G.B. Wolff (2012), "What Kind of European Banking Union?", Bruegel Policy Contribution, Bruegel, Brussels, June.

Schoenmaker, D. and D. Gros (2012), "A European Deposit Insurance and Resolution Fund", Working Document No. 364, Centre for European Policy Studies Brussels, May, later published in *Kredit & Kapital*.

Schröder, M. (2012), "Risikoübernahme im Bankensektor: Unterscheiden sich Sparkassen und Genossenschaftsbanken von Geschäftsbanken?", Zentrum für Europäische Wirtschaftsforschung (ZEW) GmbH, Mannheim.

Thies, C. and D. Gerlowski (1989): "Deposit Insurance: A History of Failure", *Cato Journal*, 8, pp. 677-693.

Van Rompuy, H., in close collaboration with J.M. Barroso, J.-C. Juncker and M. Draghi, (2012), "Towards a Genuine Economic and Monetary Union" (www.consilium.europa.eu/uedocs/cms_data/docs/pressdata/en/ec/134069.pdf).

INDEX